THE VICTORIOUS
CHRISTIAN LIFE

THE VICTORIOUS CHRISTIAN LIFE

SAMMY TIPPIT

Christian Focus

ISBN 185792 645 5

Published in 2001
by Christian Focus Publications, Geanies House,
Fearn, Ross-shire, IV20 1TW, Great Britain
Cover design by Owen Daily

Contents

PREFACE

We're living in one of the most incredible moments of human history – a time in which God has given Christians unprecedented opportunities for the proclamation of the gospel. Yet many in the church find themselves defeated in their personal walk with God. Many are prisoners to their own failures. Many are so preoccupied with their own neighbours, much less needy people around the world.

Discouragement and defeat have become the order of the day. Many sincere believers find themselves crying out regularly, 'I want victory, but don't know how to obtain it.' Many have tried and tried to overcome some besetting or secret sin, only to find themselves giving in to it. Too many followers of Christ are filled with feelings of guilt and discouragement.

But there's hope. You don't have to 'obtain' victory. It's already been purchased for you. You don't have to struggle. You don't have to keep going back to the same old sins. You don't have to wallow in the pigpen defeat. Jesus won the victory for you when he died on the cross.

You may be thinking, 'That may be true theoretically, but it's certainly not a practical reality in my life.' But it can be. I've attempted to provide you some of the great eternal truths about the victorious Christian life. I'm convinced that victory is within the grasp of every man, woman, boy and girl who has been born of the Spirit of God. Let me encourage you to make these short readings something you take into your heart and mind on a weekly basis.

You can know victory on a regular basis. It doesn't have to be something that you experience only on some rare occasion. Meditate on the great truths about the victory that Christ has for you. Appropriate them by faith on a daily basis. Allow Christ to fill you with His life. Your life can be the victorious Christian life.

Sammy Tippit

1

IS IT REALLY POSSIBLE?

One doesn't have to be a Christian for many years before he begins to wonder, "Is there really such a thing as victorious Christian living? Do I only have the promise of God's forgiveness and eternal salvation, or can I actually experience victory over old habits and ways?" I think that if we were completely honest with each other, we would discover that there are multitudes of Christians asking those questions – and for good reasons.

We only have to look around us to find many Christians living far below the victory described in the New Testament. I have often met people with such immense problems and difficulties that I've even thought there's no workable solution to their situation. Then, I look around, even among many Christian leaders, and often I find defeat, discouragement and despair throughout the Christian community. Defeat has become such a norm in the Christian community that many have given up on the Biblical principles of victory and turned to psychological and humanistic principles rather than Biblical ones. An entire industry of counselling has grown up in recent years because of so much defeat in the Christian community. Consequently, the natural tendency is to question whether victory actually exists.

Far worse than seeing the defeat of so many Christians around us is seeing our own failures. Many Christians find themselves held captive to lust, bitterness, anger, anxiety, and a host of other heart attitudes that they thought they would no longer have to face once they became a Christian. Most of us don't need to be told that we're defeated. We face that reality every day. Recently, one Christian lady very nonchalantly told me that she had been involved sexually with another woman's husband. The manner in which she confessed her sin conveyed no hope of victory over the relationship. Years ago, I confronted a pastor about an immoral relationship. He told me, "I've prayed and asked God to deliver me from these feelings that I have for this woman. But He hasn't done it. Therefore, I've accepted the relationship as what He wants for me." Too many Christians have accepted defeat as the destiny of the believer because they can't seem to get a grip on the source and way of victory in their lives.

I've often heard Christians quote the Scriptures to excuse their lack of victory in the Christian life. Most notably, King David is cited for his failure. Such reasoning states that "he was, after all, a man after God's own heart. Yet, he succumbed to lust, adultery and murder. If he was a man of God and a leader in the kingdom of God, then why should we expect to do any better than him?" The Bible is certainly filled with a multitude of examples of godly men who wound up defeated. The Apostle Paul said, "For the good that I wish, I do not do; but I practice the very evil that I do not wish" (Rom. 7:19 NASV). Peter denied Jesus, and Thomas doubted him. Abraham was a coward when a king wanted his wife. Moses fled into the Midianite desert in defeat and fear of the Pharaoh. Take a quick tour of the Bible and one could easily think that victory for the believer just doesn't exist.

But there's one other reason that many followers of Christ have stayed in the sewer of defeat. They know that the place where they're living stinks. They know that the Bible describes a different kind of life. Many want out of the slums of sin, but have accepted their ghetto dwellings as their spiritual destiny. What many people don't understand is that there's an illegitimate and evil landlord that's convinced them they must dwell in the slums. They've believed the lies of Satan. He's been telling the same old story since the creation of man. He's attempted to convince every generation of believers that they were destined to live in the slums of sin and that spiritual sewerage is the norm for the Christian life.

Victorious Christian living is certainly impossible for us in our own strength and power. Left to ourselves we will remain defeated. But there's good news for the true follower of Christ. Jesus said that "the things impossible with men are possible with God" (Luke 18:27 NASV). Our God is a God who specializes in the impossible. He's made full provision for our victory. Victorious Christian living isn't just a dream or unattainable wish for the Christian. It's a present reality. It's not something that's achievable. It's that which has *already* been achieved by Christ.

Jesus defeated every one of our enemies when He died on the cross. Foremost, He defeated Satan. The devil is described as the accuser of the brethren. He constantly tells us that there's no hope. He convinces us that defeat is our destiny. But he's a liar. The Scripture clearly tells us, "But in all these things, we overwhelmingly conquer through Him Who loved us" (Rom. 8:37 NASB). The Bible says that Jesus made a public display of the defeat of Satan when He died on the cross (Col. 2:15). We no longer have to believe the devil's lies. The victory has already been achieved over the spiritual forces in heavenly places. That's a fact.

Perhaps the most difficult struggle we face is within our own selves. That's primarily what the Apostle Paul wrestled with in Romans chapter 7. He wanted victory, but confessed that in his own self (flesh) dwelt no good thing (Rom. 7:18). He even asked the question, "Who will set me free from this body of death?" (Rom. 7:24 NASB)? He then answered his own question firmly stating, "Thanks be to God through Jesus Christ, our Lord!" (Rom. 7:25 NASB). Yes, Paul had tasted defeat. But he also knew the source of victory was found in Christ.

That's perhaps the greatest truth that I've ever learned since becoming a Christian. The victorious Christian life is not something that I can attain. It's that which Christ has obtained for me. It's not what I can do for Him, but what He's already done for me. It's not "I", but it's "Christ in me" that's the great hope of victory. My responsibility is to trust in Him. Just as I trusted Jesus to save and forgive me, I can trust Him to give me victory over every evil desire with which I am tempted. *Christ is my victory*. Yes, victorious Christian living is possible. It's attainable because Jesus has won the victory. We simply need to trust Him.

2

VICTORY – TRYING OR TRUSTING?

When I came to know Christ over 30 years ago, my life changed radically. God set me free from the immorality and selfishness that had enslaved me for so many years. I was thrilled with what God had done in my life. There were many habits that I longed to overcome, but had no power over them. However, when Jesus came into my heart, I was truly set free.

But after several months of following Christ, I noticed one habit that didn't seem to go away. I was extremely jealous. When a boy would talk to my girlfriend, anger would rise up within me. I was so enraged that I wanted to hit the guy. But I knew that was wrong and these feelings were not pleasing to God. Therefore, I decided that I needed to try real hard not to be jealous. I don't know if you've ever tried not to be jealous, but let me give you some friendly advice. Don't try. It's impossible!

The harder I tried not to be jealous, the more jealous I became. I would grit my teeth and muster all of the strength I could find, but I became even more jealous. I didn't know what to do. I tried even harder and failed even more miserably. The harder I tried to overcome this besetting sin, it seemed as though the more enslaved that I became to it.

One day I learned the secret of victorious Christian living. It's not in trying, but in trusting. It's not in what I can do, but in what Christ has already done to acquire the victory. All I needed to do was to trust in Him. He was tempted in every way in which I or anyone else has been tempted, but He was without sin. In other words, He has already overcome jealousy. I just needed to trust Him. He was living in me, and He would do the same thing today that He did 2000 years ago. I just needed to stop trying and start trusting – believing Jesus to be my victory over jealousy. The same Jesus who saved me and forgave my sins is quite capable of securing my victory over the sin that plagues me.

The next time that I felt jealousy and anger rising in my heart, I whispered a prayer, "God, just as I trusted You to save me, I'm trusting You to be my victory over jealousy and anger today." The most amazing thing happened. The feelings of insecurity and anger left. But not long after that I was tempted again to become jealous. I simply turned again to Jesus and said, "Lord, I'm trusting You again to be my victory." And victory followed.

Satan kept returning and tempting, but I kept trusting and looking unto Jesus. After several months, I began to notice that Satan wasn't tempting me nearly as often. He must have been wearied at having to deal with Jesus rather than me. Jesus has defeated the devil in our lives. The victory that we experience over temptation, sin and the devil is not in trying in the power of our own flesh. Satan knows the futility of our flesh. He knows every one of our weaknesses. He knows where we are vulnerable. That's why it's so important to trust completely in Christ and not in ourselves.

The victory has been secured by Jesus when He lived an absolutely perfect, sinless life 2000 years ago. When

He died on the cross, He declared, "It is finished." He had completed the work. He was obedient completely unto death. He made a public display of the defeat of all of the forces of evil. Three days later He arose from the grave. He overcame every enemy that man will ever face. He overcame sin, death, hell and the devil and his demons. The victory is completely His triumph. We simply enter into His triumph as we trust in Him.

The greatest lesson any believer will ever learn about victorious Christian living is that it's not in trying, but in trusting that we experience success. Trying to overcome sin in our own power is like a lion facing a den of Daniels or a Goliath facing 100 young faith-filled Davids. That would be utter defeat. But the faith of a small David can defeat any giant in our lives. Daniel trusted in God, and the lions were rendered powerless. David only met failure when he operated in the power of his flesh. Samson lost his strength when he flirted with temptation. Their only victory and strength was in the same place that you and I have victory. When they trusted in God, they were overwhelmingly more than conquerors through Christ who loved them. Stop trying and start trusting!

3

FAITH AND VICTORY

There doesn't have to be losers on Christ's side. From the richest to the poorest, from the oldest to the youngest, and from the educated to the uneducated, we all have the same source of victory. It's not our material possessions, our natural wisdom, nor our credentials. Victory is available to each of us because of what Christ has already done for us. It's His victory. He won the battle. Our victory comes as we enter into His victory, and that victory can only be apprehended through faith.

If we read about the great heroes of faith, both in Biblical times and in modern history, we discover that every one of their victories came through faith. Abel worshipped by faith. Noah worked by faith. Enoch walked by faith. Abraham travelled by faith. Moses delivered the nation by faith. David slew the giant by faith. Paul preached the gospel by faith. Luther inspired a Reformation by faith. Whitefield experienced a revival by faith. Moody shook a continent by faith. Faith always has been and always will be the way the victory is obtained. The sole issue regarding our personal victory is simply the faith issue.

So, then, it's crucial that we understand the nature of faith. Is faith a funny feeling that we get when we hear an eloquent speaker, or is faith a psychological state of mind that we achieve by the power of positive thinking? Is faith a panacea for all of our problems? Can we name it and claim it? Is it possible to believe and never again be sick as some claim? What is faith and where does it come from? The answer to that question is the secret to victorious Christian living. However, I'm afraid that we've so distorted the Biblical teaching about faith that we may need another Reformation that awakens our souls to victory and once again allows the church to be the light of the world.

Faith begins with God, not ourselves. Faith isn't when we psyche ourselves into a state of belief. It's not a funny feeling. The Bible says "faith comes by hearing, and hearing by the word of Christ." Faith doesn't begin within us. It begins with God. It's impossible to please God without faith, but it's also impossible to have faith without God. Faith is objective. It begins with a source outside of us. It begins with God speaking. It begins with the Word of God. It's an assurance in our hearts that's produced by our hearing the Word of God.

Faith begins with God speaking to our hearts His Word. It's then redirected towards God through Jesus, the Christ. Genuine Biblical faith is always directed towards Jesus. Hebrews 12:2 says, "Looking unto Jesus, the author and perfecter of our faith." Jesus is the initiator and maintainer of our faith. He is "the way, the truth, and the life." Jesus is referred to in the gospel of John as the Word of God. Therefore, any faith that doesn't begin and continue with Him isn't true faith.

Many Christians find themselves defeated because they've trusted in themselves, their abilities, their financial holdings, or even their experience rather than in Christ alone. Often God has to allow disability within us in order to show us His ability. He may strip us of our financial wealth in order to supply every need of ours through His riches in glory by Christ Jesus (Phil. 4:19). Our experiences can even be deceiving, but Jesus is absolute truth. Victory comes only through trusting Jesus – and Jesus alone.

Faith begins with God speaking to our hearts through His Word and continues by our looking unto Jesus to meet every need we have. But, finally, faith works. Our works don't produce faith, but rather the opposite is true. Faith produces works – the work of God in our lives. Therefore, we can't brag or boast about any of our abilities, resources, or achievements. We can only boast in Christ. He has become our total source of victory and achievement. If we are truly trusting in Christ, then we will know His victory.

Occasionally I'm challenged on that assertion. People will say to me, "Sammy, I've trusted in Christ, but it just didn't help." As I probe them, however, I discover that their trust was more in their own efforts and expertise, rather than in the sufficiency and power of Christ. I have been on this journey of walking with Jesus for more than 35 years now, and there's one thing that I can say with absolute conviction – "I've failed Jesus many times, but He's never once failed me."

I've discovered this great truth – victory in the Christian life comes only through faith. Faith begins by beholding God speaking to us through Jesus, the Word of God. It continues by looking unto Jesus, and it concludes with victory – not ours but His. We simply enter into the victory that He's already won. It was not that Noah, Abraham, Moses, David, Paul, Luther and Whitefield were so great. It was simply that they trusted in a great and mighty God. They looked unto Jesus. It's magnificent to ponder the thought that the God of Abraham, Moses, David, Paul, Luther, and Moody is our God. It's not our great abilities that will usher in the victory, but it's simple faith in a mighty God that brings forth the victory.

4

ASSURANCE OF SALVATION

One of the greatest hindrances to victorious Christian living is the lack of assurance of one's salvation. If we continually doubt God's forgiveness in our lives, Satan renders us ineffective. I've met many Christians who long for victory, but seem to always find themselves struggling and defeated. If there's no security in our relationship to God, then defeat is assured and victory is only a passing dream.

Many years ago, I had a friend who continually struggled with God's acceptance of him even though he had come to know Christ. He grew up in an abusive home. His father was an alcoholic and often beat the children when he was in a drunken stupor. Consequently, when my friend became a Christian, he had a distorted view of God as his father. Any time that he did something wrong, he felt rejected by God and feared what might happen to him. One day a Christian leader began to disciple my friend. He not only taught him the truths of God's Word, but he also was a living example of those truths.

He showed grace to my friend when he failed. He didn't berate him, but he encouraged him. When he fell spiritually, he picked him up. My friend began to experience more and more victory in his life daily. I didn't see my friend for many years after that. Not long ago, he was visiting the city where I live. He called me and wanted to get together for a meal. The change in his life was incredible. He was secure. He no longer was trying to get everyone's acceptance. He knew that he was accepted by God, and that had released him to grow and mature in Christ.

The Bible calls Satan "the accuser of the brethren." He accuses us to God. He accuses us to our fellow believers. But most of the damage inflicted upon us comes when we believe his accusations about us. We become what we believe. If we believe what God says, we find ourselves growing in the grace and knowledge of Christ. If we believe the accusation of the devil, we become defeated.

I'm not speaking about the new "name it and claim it" theology. I'm speaking of the old time, old fashioned "standing on the promises of God" theology. God's Word says, "These things have I written unto you who believe on the name of the Son of God, so that you may know that you have eternal life" (1 John 5:13). The Bible says that we can *know* that we have eternal life – not hope, wish, or think that we have eternal life. We can rest in the absolute assurance that we are the children of God – not because of anything that we have done, but because of His grace.

The verse immediately prior to the one just quoted tells us how we can know for sure that we have eternal life. It says, "He who has the Son has life" (1 John 5:12). How do we know that we have eternal life? If we have the Son of God in our lives, then we can rest in the firm certainty that we have that eternal life because God's Word says we do. We must then learn to stand on the promises of God.

Victory flows from a secure relationship with God. It comes from standing on the eternal promises of God's Word. It's the practical knowledge of the wonderful love of the Father for His children. That's why the Bible says that "we are more than conquerors through Christ who loved us." We're not simply victors. We are *"more than conquerors."*

When we comprehend this great truth, we begin to soar with the eagles. There's a confidence that permeates our character. Winners are always confident – not over-confident. Just confident. Winners know their potential. That's settled in their hearts and minds. As believers in Jesus Christ, our potential for victory in the Christian life is unlimited because Jesus has secured the victory for us. We walk in His victory, not ours. Victory comes from a fixed future in heaven, a safe relationship with the Saviour on earth, and a confident conviction about our position in Christ. The most secure place in the world to live is in Christ and to know that He is living in us. That's the blessed assurance that we have.

5

DEALING WITH DOUBTS

Often I'm asked, "Do you ever have doubts about God?" Most people are surprised to hear that a Christian author, international evangelist, and a follower of Christ for 36 years still struggles with doubts. But I do. I learned a long time ago that it's not sin to doubt your beliefs. It becomes sin when you believe your doubts.

Early in my Christian life, I found myself doubting often. I would do something that I knew didn't please God, and heart-searching questions always followed my sin. "How could you do that and really be a Christian? If there's a God, then why do these things keep happening?"

A few days after becoming a Christian, I found myself in my room crying out to God. Doubts flooded my soul. "Is there a God? Have you been brainwashed? Have you simply had an emotional experience?" I felt so confused. I called on God. It seemed like the only words I could say in those moments were, "Jesus, Oh Jesus, help me!" After crying out to God for several minutes, peace like a river flooded my soul. The Holy Spirit bore witness with my spirit that I was the child of God. I knew that I knew that Christ was real. It was deeper than emotion and broader than human understanding. It was a spiritual knowledge.

The Christian life is like a journey. All along the way, you make discoveries. You continue to learn and grow. The person who does not grow always ends up defeated.

Many of the greatest discoveries about the Christian life have come as I've had to deal with doubts. I've learned to let doubt lead me to new heights of faith rather than force me to the depths of despair. I've also learned to identify the source of doubts.

Before I came to know Christ, the source of my doubts was deep. They were of a profoundly spiritual nature. They went to the core of my being. I doubted because I had no vital relationship with God. I didn't have the assurance of God because I had no knowledge of God. God is Spirit. His Spirit wasn't present in my life.

But after becoming a believer, the doubts that I experienced were only surface. The deepest part of mankind is the spirit of man. I no longer doubted on that level because "His Spirit bears witness with my spirit that I am a child of God" (Rom. 8:16). In other words, in the deepest part of my being I know that I am a child of God because the Holy Spirit lives in the deepest part of my heart.

He continually tells me that I'm God's child, that the blood of Christ is sufficient provision to cleanse me of all my sins. This isn't merely positional theology, but it's practical reality. Hallelujah! God's Spirit dwells deep within and continually tells me that I belong to Jesus and He belongs to me! I just know that I know that I know. It's deep down in my heart, and I just know it. It's not simply some kind of intellectual knowledge or an emotional feeling. It's spiritual. It's His presence in my life.

Then, what about the doubts? Where do they come from? Even though I have that deep assurance that Jesus is mine, I still have to deal with surface doubts. Those doubts come from areas of my life such as the intellectual and emotional. For instance, when I disobey God, it always leaves an intellectual or emotional scar on my inner being. I begin to question whether I am truly God's child. Even though I know in the deepest part of my heart that Christ's death on the cross is sufficient for my forgiveness, my reasoning often becomes scarred. I begin to doubt mentally that I'm a child of God. Or I may feel emotionally defeated and thus doubt whether I truly have eternal life. Once the sin has been confessed and I've truly repented, then I again rest in the confidence of Christ's salvation. The doubts were only surface. Thus, they were also temporary.

Intellectual doubts normally stem from an incorrect view of God, while emotional doubts often come from wrong actions and attitudes. Rather than believing what the Bible says about God and us, we often believe what our culture teaches us about Him. Consequently, we become defeated. Every victory we experience in Christ emanates from faith. Faith is the foundation upon which victory is built in the Christian's life. But the faith foundation can't be built upon anything but the truth of God's Word. We must stand on the promises of the Bible if we are to practically experience victory over doubts.

Intellectual doubts flow from a lack of knowledge of God's Word, but emotional doubts are often caused by disobedience to the Word of God. By faith in Christ, we enter into a relationship with God. We become His child. However, when we allow sin into our lives, our intimacy with Him is broken. We no longer experience practically the depth, width, breadth and height of His love. His love for us hasn't changed. We are still His children, but our fellowship with Him has been shattered. That fellowship can only be restored when we confess and repent of our sins. It's only when travelling down the highway of

29

holiness that we have intimacy with God, who is absolute holiness.

When we believe what God says about us and live and act upon those great truths, we will experientially know that we are His children. Doubts will disappear. Faith will grow. And victory will be our battle cry. We will know what it means to be victors.

6

KNOWING GOD THROUGH PRAYER

Victory in the Christian life flows from an intimate knowledge of God. If you had asked me soon after I first met my wife, "Do you know a young lady named Debe "Tex" Sirman?", I would have responded, "Yes, I know her. I met her the other day." However, what I meant when I said that I knew her then and when I say that I know her today are two entirely different things. I have an intimate knowledge of her that I didn't have at that time. I now know her likes and dislikes, her strengths and weaknesses, and her joys and sorrows.

When we first began seeing each other, I knew that I loved her. However, the love that I have for her today is so much deeper – so much richer. Because we've walked together in many situations and faced many different circumstances, our love has grown immensely. The same is true with God. The more that you get to know Him, the more that you love Him. As we walk with Him in the valleys as well as on the mountain tops, our love intensifies for Him. But it takes time to get to know Him.

The Apostle Paul wrote that the deep longing of his heart was that he might "know Him (Christ), and the power of His resurrection and the fellowship of His sufferings, being made conformable to His death" (Phil. 3:10). Paul wanted to get to know Christ on the mountain tops and in the valleys. He wanted to walk with Christ through the tough times as well as the good times because he knew that his relationship with Christ would grow only in the garden of such longterm intimacy.

But on a practical level, how do we really get to know God? How do we experience His love and care? God is Spirit. Therefore, how do we have such a deep relationship with God whom we cannot see or touch? One way in which we develop that intimacy with Christ is through prayer.

Many people only see prayer as a way to get something from God. It's certainly true that God gives abundantly to His children as a result of our requests. In fact, He's able to give us abundantly far above anything that we could ask or even think of asking. But prayer is so much more than obtaining what we want from Him. Prayer is the communion of two hearts. It's our communicating with God the intimate things of our lives, and His communicating with us the deep things of His heart.

Too many of us are defeated in our Christian lives because we've had the wrong understanding of what prayer really is. We view prayer as a time in which we go to the "great Santa Claus in the sky" and tell Him all the things that we want. Such a shallow view of prayer can only lead to defeat. We can't run in and out of the presence of the holy, almighty God as we would run into a department store with our shopping list.

Any healthy relationship takes time. My wife and I have developed a wonderful and deep relationship over the years because we've taken time to communicate with each other what's really on our hearts. We attempt every week to find a time and place to get away from the phone, the office, and any other distractions. We take that time to share our hearts with each other. We share our problems, our hurts, our difficulties, and our victories that we've experienced during the week. Our most difficult moments in our relationship have come when we haven't taken the time to communicate.

The same is true with prayer. It takes time to really communicate with God and for Him to communicate with us what's deep within His heart. Perhaps that's why Jesus told His disciples that when they prayed, they were to go into their closets and shut the door and that the Father who hears in secret would reward them publicly (Matt. 6: 6). Prayer is not a religious show whereby we attempt to impress others with our spirituality. It's not a religious duty or obligation. Prayer is first and foremost a time whereby we get away from the hustle and bustle of life so that we can share the intimate things of our hearts with God. It's taking time to listen to His voice. It's communion with the Creator of the universe.

Often I'm challenged on this principle. Some will say, "We should always be in a spirit of prayer. Therefore, we don't need to set aside a time to be alone with God." It's true that we are to "pray without ceasing." We should attempt to maintain a spirit of prayer throughout our daily lives. However, that doesn't mean that we don't need a regular consistent time to get alone with God and develop that intimate communication. Jesus taught His disciples to do that. If they needed to find a time and a place to get away from the distractions of the world and commune with God, then how much more do we need that time and place.

If you really desire victory in your Christian life, this could be a starting place for you. It's certainly not all there is to victory, but it's a great starting place. Why don't you find a place and set aside a time where you meet with God? Tell Him what's on your heart. Read His Word and listen to His voice. Determine that you will obey whatever He says to you. You'll find victory there.

7

LORD, TEACH US TO PRAY

The disciples had seen Jesus do many incredible works. They watched Him turn water into wine, heal the sick, cast out evil spirits, preach a great sermon, and even raise the dead. Yet, they never asked Him to teach them to do any of those things. However, they did say, "Lord, teach us to pray" (Luke 11:1). They knew that the secret to all of His great deeds was His prayer life. He would spend long periods of time during the early hours of the morning in prayer. They wanted in on His secret of victory.

Jesus taught the disciples in the following verses how to pray. A parallel passage is found in Matthew 6:9-13. In that passage Jesus teaches five principles of prayer. Each one could be summarized as a response to a particular attribute of God. Prayer is getting to know God. As we see Him in all of His splendour and glory, we begin to pour our hearts out to Him. Prayer then becomes the greatest adventure upon which anyone could embark. I'm often asked what a person does when He prays. People often feel that they wouldn't know what to do for thirty minutes or an hour of prayer. However, when we begin to practise these principles, often people find that they need more time to pray.

So, then how should we pray, and what are the principles that Jesus taught?

The first principle is the *principle of praise and thanksgiving*. Jesus opens the door of prayer in Matthew

6:9 with the focus upon God. He teaches the disciples to look at three attributes of God: *a) Our father; b) which art in heaven; c) hallowed be thy name.* The fatherhood of God shows us the goodness of God. That's especially important for us to understand when difficult things take place in our lives. We need to understand that God is good and only wants the best for our lives. He won't give us a stone when we ask for bread. In fact, if the world or the devil gives us a stone, He will turn it into bread.

The phrase, "which art in heaven", shows us the greatness of God. He's on His throne. He has all power and authority in heaven and on earth. He is the Almighty God. But Jesus shows us the holiness of God in the phrase, "hallowed be thy Name." God is in a category all His own. We are the creation. He is the Creator. We are sinful. He is absolute purity. There is none anywhere in the universe like Him. Therefore, we should bow before Him in reverence.

We thank God for His goodness – all of the many good things that He's done for us. We praise Him for who He is – His attributes and character. Therefore, when we pray, first take some time to focus on who God is and what He's done for us. Worship Him in the beauty of His holiness. Thank Him for His mighty works in our lives.

The second principle found in Matthew 6:10 is the *principle of intercession.* After Jesus points the disciples to the attributes of God, He then shows them the needs of the world. The focus shifts from God to His kingdom and His will on earth. As we get to know God, we will begin to desire what's on His heart. And what is on God's heart? That hasn't changed in 2000 years. The world is on God's heart (John 3:16)! We should begin to pray for people who need Christ, that God's kingdom would come and that His will would be done in their lives. This is the most powerful kind of praying that I know because it goes straight to the heart of God. God will move heaven to earth when we come in agreement with His heart, His kingdom, and His will.

The third principle is that of *supplication* (Matt. 6:11). Jesus taught His disciples to bring their needs to God when He taught them to ask God for daily bread. Food is the most basic need of humanity. Jesus wants His disciples to know God as Jehovah Jireh, God their provider. God is desiring to meet the needs of His children. He loves us and will take care of us. Every day we ought to bring our needs to God. He bids us to do that.

Notice the order in which Jesus taught His disciples to pray. First, their focus is only on God. Then, the focus shifts to His kingdom coming to the Earth. We pray for others. Finally, we bring our own needs to God. The priorities in prayer that Jesus taught his disciples were – God first, others second, and our own needs third. Most of us pray in the opposite manner.

Once we begin to bring our needs to God, then Jesus leads us to the deepest concerns of our hearts, those that are spiritual needs. The fourth principle is that of *forgiveness*, which is a response to the holiness and grace of God. This principle, which is stated in Matt. 6:12, teaches us that we must rely upon God for His grace and forgiveness in our own lives. We must draw from that deep well of grace in order to forgive others. There are two heart problems that produce defeat in our prayer lives – guilt and bitterness. Jesus deals with both in this passage of Scripture.

Finally, Jesus teaches the disciples how to engage in

spiritual warfare in Matthew 6:13. We look to Jesus as the Great Shepherd who leads our lives into a place of safety and away from the temptations of this world. We also look to Him as our victory over the forces and power of evil. Jesus is our victory. As we follow His plan of prayer for our lives, we live in victory. Look unto Jesus. Ask Him today, "Lord, teach me to pray." You'll find victory as He teaches you.

8

PRAYER AND VICTORY

There exists an undeniable relationship between the life of prayer and the victorious Christian life. If one were to take a journey throughout the history of the church, he would discover that the great giants of the faith were men and women of prayer. If we travel all the way back to the New Testament church, we would find a small band of fishermen, tax collectors, doubters, and common ordinary Jewish followers of Christ turning the Roman empire upside down. They shook the world because they stood in reverent silence in the presence of God. They were a people of prayer. It was one of the great characteristics of the church in the book of Acts.

But it's not just the recent historical church and the first century believers that found their victory through prayer. Even the ancient Hebrew leaders rose or fell because of their prayer or lack of prayer lives. One glaring example is that of Uzziah. He was only sixteen when he became king (2 Chron. 26:1). How would a teenager be able to assume the responsibilities of the kingdom? He would be the bottom line leader – answerable for the economy, for transportation, housing, and the general well-being of Judah. It seemed like an impossible task for such a young person.

However, Uzziah was wise. He understood one great truth that was enough to make him a successful leader. He didn't know much as a young person, but he knew the One who was the source of all knowledge. Therefore, he cast himself on the mercy and grace of God. The Bible says, "He sought God during the days of Zechariah, who instructed him in the fear of God. *As long as he sought the Lord, God gave him success*" (2 Chron. 26:5). His victory rested in his humility. He knew that he didn't have the ability to lead the people, but he knew that with God nothing was impossible.

However, something happened as Uzziah experienced victory. It was a subtle but deadly danger. The Bible describes the ultimate defeat that came to Uzziah, "But after Uzziah became powerful, his pride led to his downfall...." When Uzziah was young and knew nothing, he had to be completely dependent upon God. However, when he became strong, he felt he no longer needed to pray. He thought that he knew how to run the kingdom by himself, and his pride led to his defeat.

Uzziah's experience isn't so unusual. I've found that the most dangerous times in my life often follow my greatest victories. There comes a smug sense of "I've got it under control." The truth is that I don't have it under control. God has it under control, and I had better continue to seek His face and leadership in everything that I do. Prayer is the outward expression of a humble heart. Prayer says, "Oh, God, I need You. Without You, I can do nothing." However, a prayerless life says, "I can do it in my own power. I know how to do this. I've been successful many times before. I can do it myself."

Often when we're young in the Lord, we have a keen sense of our need for God. We depend upon Him, and He gives us victory. We seek God in prayer. Our hearts pant after God as the deer pants for water. We're hungry – thirsty to know and walk in victory. But after a time of victory, we begin to think that we can live the Christian life in our own power. Once that attitude has crept into our hearts, we are surely headed for a fall – just as sure as Uzziah fell, so will we.

That's why prayer is so important to us. It's not just some religious ritual that God expects us to perform. It's a heart crying out to God, "I need you!" Prayer is setting aside time to commune with the Creator and Sustainer of the universe. It's the heart longing for an intimate knowledge of our Redeemer. Prayer is getting to know God. There is no victory outside that knowledge. But I'm convinced that as long as we seek the Lord, God will give us success. He did it with Uzziah. He did it with the New Testament Church. He's done it with the great men and women of faith throughout the centuries. And He'll do it with us. He's not changed, and His ways have not changed.

9

RELATING TO GOD THROUGH HIS WORD

In the early 1990s, I went to the Republic of Mongolia to teach the small band of believers in the nation the principles of prayer that I had written in my book, *The Prayer Factor*. Mongolia had never received the gospel since the inception of Christianity. Missionaries long ago had gone there, but had been rebuffed. For the last 2000 years no one had heard the wonderful message of God's salvation.

Although the nation was predominantly Buddhist, the communists had wiped out all belief in God. But when freedoms began to come to the nation, the doors began to open for the gospel. A small group of people in the capital city of Ulan Batar came to believe in Jesus. I was asked to go there and teach them on prayer. I taught principles of prayer for several evenings. God moved wonderfully during the meetings. At the close of the meetings in Ulan Batar, I was asked to go to another city, Darhan. There were no believers in that city at that time. The people had never even heard of Jesus.

After I shared the good news of who God is and what He can do in our lives, an old man asked me a very significant question. He inquired, "What does your God look like?" I was somewhat taken back. No one had ever asked me such a question. How would you have answered that question? It was one of the most difficult questions that I've ever had to answer.

But basically I said to the old man, "If you want to know

what God looks like, then you need to know that He has given us a book that describes His nature, character, and attributes. That book was written by holy men who were inspired by God. They lived during different periods of history. Some were kings. Others were ordinary fishermen. But all had encountered the God who created the universe. They wrote of His deeds and the testimonies, and of how God had changed their lives. They told of His laws and principles of life." My answer seemed to satisfy the old man.

If you want to really know God intimately, then you need to understand that there is an objective testimony of who He is and how He works. The Bible is God's Word to His people. If we truly want to get to know God and learn to live in harmony with Him, then we need to commit ourselves to reading, studying, and meditating on His Word. There's a fourfold purpose in our taking the Word of God into our lives on a regular daily basis.

The Apostle Paul wrote to young Timothy and explained what the Scriptures can do in our lives. He said, "All Scripture is God breathed, and is useful for teaching, rebuking, correcting, and training in righteousness, so that the man of God may be thoroughly equipped for every good work" (2 Tim. 3:16). Paul lists how God deals with the negative as well as the positive things in our lives. First, he tells us how the Scriptures will teach us – we learn who God is and how we can know and walk with Him. Second, the Bible rebukes us when there are areas of our lives that don't please God. The Bible becomes our ultimate source of authority and accountability. God draws the parameters around our lives and then lets us know if we have crossed those boundaries.

But God doesn't just tell us when we've done something

wrong. He corrects us – that is, He shows us in the Scriptures how to get back into the parameters of safety where we should be living. Finally, God instructs us in the ways of right living – in living in a correct and proper relationship with Him. It would be inconceivable to think that we could experience consistent victory in our lives without knowing who He is, how He works, and what He expects from us. The Bible is God's instruction manual for victorious Christian living. It's His map that guides us on the trail of triumph.

A champion will always have a plan – a strategy for winning. God has given us His strategy for a winning life. It's found in an age old book, the Bible. If you want to be a winner in the race of life, then study that book of all ages, the Bible. It's God's Word. It's His divine strategy for living and our instruction manual for training in righteousness. But most of all, it gives the fullest and most complete description of what He looks like. Read it and reap a resounding victory!

10

TAKING THE WORD OF GOD INTO OUR HEARTS

The Psalmist revealed the secret of successful Christian living when he wrote, "I have hidden Your word in my heart that I might not sin against You" (Ps. 119:11). Jesus expressed the same conviction when He told His disciples, "Man does not live on bread alone, but on every word that comes from the mouth of God" (Matt. 4:4). There's an internal hunger within every one of us that cries out for the Bread of life. That hunger and thirst can only be filled when we take in God's provision for the deepest hungers of our hearts. Otherwise, we become spiritually weak and eventually fall into despair and defeat. We must take the Word of God into our lives if we are to experience victory in our daily walk with Christ.

But on a practical level, how do we do that? Over the years of walking with Christ, I've learned five ways in which we can take in God's Word to our lives. First, we need to *read the Word of God.* Jesus said, "You are already clean because of the word I have spoken to you" (John 15:3). The Word of God has a cleansing effect upon our lives as we read it. It's important that we read the Scriptures systematically, regularly, and devotionally. As we read it methodically, we will begin to see the nature of God. We'll discover what's on His heart. We'll learn who He is and how He works. But we need also to read it regularly. We couldn't survive if we didn't eat physically on a regular basis. Then what makes us think that we can survive spiritually if we don't eat God's spiritual food on a regular basis?

But we, also, need to read the Bible devotionally. That means that we take the Word of God into our lives through *meditating on the Word.* As we read the Scriptures, we need to think on them. The Bible can't be read like it's just any other book. The Bible is the Word of God. It's how God speaks to our hearts. Therefore, we need time to assimilate what we've read into our minds, emotions, and actions. We need to think about what we've read and then apply it to our lives. It helps if we begin our day by reading the Scriptures. Then as we drive, walk, work, or study throughout the day, we can meditate on what God has said to us.

A third way in which we can take the Word of God into our lives is by hearing the Word of God. Paul wrote, "Faith comes from hearing the message, and the message is heard through the word of Christ" (Rom. 10:17). That's an amazing statement. Have you ever wondered how you could develop more faith or grow in your faith? Paul clearly states that such growth comes by hearing the Word of Christ.

Several years ago I was preaching in two cities in Peru. In the first city, the sports arena was about two-thirds full. I preached a clear and simple message about God's plan of salvation for our lives. There were about the same number of people in attendance in the second city as the first one, but there was one major difference. There were many more people who responded to the message to give their hearts to Christ in the second city than there were in the first one. I wondered why that had happened. In both places, people

48

had prayed. There were about the same number of non-Christians attending the meetings in both cities. Then, I remembered that in the first city we had problems with the sound system. The people in the first city couldn't hear the Word of God proclaimed nearly as clearly as in the second city. There was a very distinct sound in the second city. At that moment a great truth occurred to me. Faith comes only when we hear clearly and distinctly the Word of God. How we hear the Word of God determines how able we are to respond in faith.

There's a fourth way in which we can take the Scriptures into our lives – *memorize the Word of God.* This enables us to grow in several ways. First, when we learn by heart the Scriptures, it enables us to more ably apply the Word of God to our lives in a moment of need. We've tucked it into the inner recesses of our soul. Just at the moment when we need a promise, a command, or a testimony, God's provision through His Word comes to our mind. Thus, we are enabled to renew our minds. We can bring every thought "captive unto the obedience of Christ" (2 Cor. 10:5). Second, we are enabled to give an answer upon every occasion to the questions about our faith. Consequently, we become more courageous in sharing our faith.

Finally, we need to *study the Word of God.* The Apostle Paul told young Timothy, "Do your best to present yourself to God as one approved, a workman who does not need to be ashamed and who correctly handles the word of truth" (2 Tim. 2:15). There are several ways in which we can study the Bible. However, no matter which way we study the Scriptures, we must always have a heart to encounter God in them. Study, not just to get intellectual understanding, but study to get to know God better. One

49

of the greatest times of personal growth in my spiritual life came from doing a character study on the life of Moses. I met with God during that study, and He was able to change the direction of my life.

There are other types of studies to which you can give yourself. You can do an expository study – a verse by verse or book by book study of the Bible. Or you can have a topical study of the Bible – a study on the grace of God, or prayer or some other subject. Another manner in which you can study the Bible is a word study. Study the original meanings of the words used in the Bible. No matter which way you approach the study of the Scriptures, just make sure that you're doing it with a heart that's hungry to know God.

The Bible says that God spoke to Moses "face to face, as a man speaks with his friend" (Ex. 33:11). God wants to speak to you just as personally as He did with Moses. The way He does that is through His Word. If you want God to share with you what's on His heart, then you must take the Word of God into your life. When God speaks, you will be made clean, and you'll begin to walk in victory.

11

VICTORIOUS OBEDIENCE TO THE WORD OF GOD

Victory in the Christian life doesn't begin within us. It's not our ability to pull ourselves up by our bootstraps and live in the manner which pleases God. It's God enabling us by His grace to live the way we ought to live. We live by faith in God and not ourselves. It's absolute dependence upon Him. Yet, there's a distinct correlation between faith and obedience. Both contain elements of the will. Faith is a volitional choice, while obedience is the outworking action of that choice.

Jesus described those who love Him when He said, "he who has my commandments and keeps them is he who loves Me" (John 14:21). It's easy to say that we love Jesus, but the evidence of our love for Him lies within our obedience to Him. We can sing our songs of love and worship, but if they are not accompanied with obedience to His word then we're just playing some sort of a religious game. To love God is to obey God. Obedience is more than saying that I love someone. It's reaching out through concrete actions to that person.

If I were a rancher and needed to build a fence to keep in the cattle, it would be an act of love for my son to say to me, "Dad, I'd like to help you build that fence." It would be great to hear him say, "Dad, I love you." That would mean a great deal to me. But if he went a step further and said, "Dad, I love you, and because of that, I want to pitch in and help you build that fence," then that would be a great expression of his love for me.

Jesus has given us commandments. There's a way of life for the Christian. It's the walk of obedience. There's a very interesting thing that takes place when we obey the Word of God. God makes Himself known to us. He discloses Himself to us. In other words, obedience breeds the knowledge of God, and the knowledge of God produces victory. It's cyclic. The more we obey the Word of God, the more we're enabled to live a life of victory.

The opposite is also true. When we disobey God, then our fellowship with Him is broken. If we continue to live in disobedience, then we find ourselves going deeper and deeper in the sinking sands of sin. It becomes more and more difficult to walk in victory. Spiritual strongholds are built in areas of our hearts. Brick by brick, disobedient act by disobedient act, Satan is able to build a fortress in our hearts. We eventually find ourselves captive to degrading desires and secret sins. Defeat begins to describe the spiritual condition of our lives.

There's only one way out of the prison that's been built around our lives. Brick by brick, we must tear down the fortress. One act of obedience by another act of obedience, we will begin to see God's light and experience victory. We need not be discouraged by one moment of failure. God has given us clear instructions. He says, "If we confess our sins, He is faithful and just to forgive us our sins and cleanse us from all unrighteousness" (1 John 1:9). When we admit that we've been wrong and turn from that wrong, then God will forgive us, pick us up, and enable us to walk with Him once again.

When my son, Dave, was about one year old, he began

to attempt to walk. I'll never forget that first step. His mother and I were so proud of him. But when he took that first step, he fell down. Now, I didn't fuss at him. I didn't say, "What are you doing? Why are you so clumsy?" No. I encouraged him to get up and try again.

Sure he cried a little. But he got back up and tried to take another step. He kept doing that until he successfully made that first step. Then he tried to take a few steps. He fell again. But he got back up and continued to try to walk. Soon, he was walking everywhere – then running – then jumping. It wasn't long until walking and running became a natural function of his life.

The same is true in our Christian life. Yes, there will be times of failure. But never forget that God is pulling for you. He's on your team. He wants you to walk successfully. He's standing there saying, "Come on, get up. You can do it." He reaches His hand out to help us up and says, "Now, take another step." The more we do that, the more victory we experience. Soon, walking in victory becomes a supernatural natural way of life. It becomes the norm. Perhaps, that's why the old hymn writer said, "Trust and obey. For there's no other way to be happy in Jesus, but to trust and obey."

12

RELATING TO GOD BY
RELATING TO HIS PEOPLE

When my wife and I were living in Switzerland during the mid 1970s, we discovered that she was expecting our second child. Our daughter, Renee, was born in the middle of the Swiss Alps in a quaint little village called Château d'Oex. It's one of the most beautiful places on this planet. After she was born, we certainly would have never entertained the thought of saying to her, "Renee, we've brought you into this world. Now we're going to leave you on these mountains, and you're just going to have to grow up on your own. We've done our part. We brought you into this world. Now you need to do your part and grow up."

Those would have been unthinkable and cruel thoughts. Renee needed a family. She needed a mother and father to care for her and the security that only a family could provide. We fed her and clothed her. We provided emotional support and security. Consequently, she's grown up to be a wonderfully balanced and emotionally stable young woman.

When we are born into the kingdom of God, we need the same kind of spiritual love, security, and encouragement that a newborn child requires. Too often, new Christians attempt to mature spiritually outside the context of God's people. But God didn't create us as "Lone Rangers." He created us to function as a team – as parts of one Body. We must learn how to walk spiritually. We need to be fed the Word of God. I believe that fellowship with other Christians is one of the most important practices that the Christian must give himself to.

When God created us, He instilled a need for fellowship with others into our lives. When He saved us, He also infused into the deepest part of our souls a need for fellowship with others who have experienced God's grace. Therefore, each of us needs to find a church that preaches and teaches the Bible as God's Word. We need to find a group of people who have come to know Christ and can help us to get to know Him better.

I've been a Christian for 35 years, and I know that all churches have problems. There's no perfect church because churches are made of imperfect people. However, the church is to be an assembly of those who have come to the cross. It's not a showcase for saints, but rather a hospital for sinners. It's where we go to get our lives mended. It's a nursery that provides an atmosphere for spiritual growth. We first feast on the milk of God's Word. As we grow we are more able to digest the meat of the Scriptures.

We learn to clothe ourselves with the whole armour of God as we face the battles of life. We are able to hear the Word of God and interact with others who have heard and experienced the same great truths. The bottom line is that a good, strong Bible believing church will provide the atmosphere to become all that God intended us to become. We grow. We give. We become – all that God desires for us to become.

Fellowship with other believers is as necessary to spiritual health and life as water is to a fish; air to a bird; and food to every human being. Without it, we would soon die. I've watched many Christians wither on the vine and die spiritually because they decided that they didn't need the fellowship of other Christians any longer. Perhaps they were hurt by another believer. Or maybe they disagreed with someone in their church. They may have even seen much hypocrisy in the lives of Christians. However, forsaking fellowship with other believers is no solution to all of the above circumstances. It does no good to anyone. If we aren't comfortable with the group of believers with whom we are meeting, then we need to find another group of Bible believing Christians and grow with them. Fellowship with other Christians isn't just an option for Christian growth. It's a necessity.

13

WHERE TWO OR THREE ARE GATHERED

When I first came to know Christ, I wanted my friends to also come to know Him. I prayed for them. Not long afterwards several of them received Christ into their hearts. We began meeting together early in the morning to pray and read the Scriptures. We lived at the time in Baton Rouge, which is the capital of the state of Louisiana. Near the capital building is a hill that overlooks a lake. We would meet on that hill and then separate for a period of time to have a time alone with God. We would spend time in prayer and reading and memorizing the Scripture. We then came back together and shared what we were feeling with each other and what we felt God was saying to our hearts.

Those were some of the most precious times of my life. I look back on those days with very fond memories. Even though most of us have moved away from Baton Rouge and live elsewhere, that little spot became holy ground to us. It was a place where we met with God and He met with us. It was a special time in our lives that actually set the pattern for our growth. When I return home to visit family and friends in Baton Rouge, I always like to go by that spot near the state capital. It reminds me of the formative years of my Christian experience. But, most of all, it reminds me of my need for fellowship with others who have come to know Christ as I have come to know Him.

As I look back over the years, I've discovered that it's been a close-knit fellowship with others that has been so helpful to me in my walk with God. When I was a pastor in Germany, God gave me an attorney friend who challenged me to be all that God wanted me to be. When I travelled into Romania, God gave me a Romanian medical doctor friend who challenged me to reach the nation for Christ. He challenged me about my speaking style and method of communication.

At Sammy Tippit Ministries we have a Board of Directors to whom I am accountable with this ministry. They are a group of men who love God and love me. But they're not afraid to speak to me about the difficult things. Some time ago, I asked them to be honest with me and tell me what I needed to do to become more effective for Christ. They did! It was devastating to me (in a good sense). I needed to be broken in some areas of my life and leadership. They loved me enough to be honest with me.

It's those kind of honest and transparent relationships that enable us to become all that God intended us to become. I'm convinced that we all need a small group of people around us who love Jesus and love us – who love us enough to speak to us about the difficult things. There are three characteristics to such relationships. First, we need fellowship with people who love God – those who inspire us to love God with all of our hearts.

Second, we need fellowship with people who love us. I could accept the correction of those men because I knew that they loved me. I knew that what they had to say to me wasn't because they were angry with me or that they "wanted to put me in my place." I knew that they pointed out my blind spots because they genuinely cared about me. Finally, we need people who will be honest with us no matter how much it hurts. Not everyone will feel that they can be that open and honest. But every Christian needs someone or some group of people who will love us enough to correct us.

Jesus said that where "two or three come together in My name, there I am with them" (Matt. 18:20). If you want to experience true victory, then find two or three people who love Jesus the same way that you love Him. Meet with them on a regular basis and seek God together. Be open, honest, and vulnerable. God will work in and through you. You will grow in His grace and reach even greater levels of victory in your walk with God.

14

RESTORING BROKEN RELATIONSHIPS

We live in a world filled with broken relationships. Nations war against nations. Ethnic groups hate other ethnic groups. Gangs protect their turf. Husbands and wives divorce one another. Broken relationships are simply a sign of a generation that has rejected Christ.

I'm often asked why there are so many bad things that happen in the world if God is so good. There's a simple answer to that question. God gives us a choice. He didn't create us as robots. He made each of us "a living soul." When we choose to disobey Him and go our own way, then we reap the fruit of our independence and rebellion. Most often that fruit includes broken relationships, whether they be in families, communities, nations, or regions of the world.

The reverse is also true. When we choose to obey God and follow Christ, we begin to mend those broken relationships. We can't love God and at the same time hate our fellow man. It's impossible. A heart and life rooted and planted in the love of God will not bear the fruit of bitterness. Where there's hatred we can know that there's an absence of God's grace.

At some point in our lives, others will wrong us all. The great challenge facing the follower of Christ is how we will respond to the wrong that was thrust upon us. The secret to victory in our lives lies at the cross of Christ. There's no greater example in all of human history of a man being wronged. All of us have sinned and done wrong things. But He never sinned. He was perfect in every way. He obeyed God completely. He loved as no other man has ever loved. He lived life the way life is to be lived. Yet, He was nailed to an old rugged cross. He was spat upon, laughed at, beaten, and crucified. Yet, He cried out, "Father, forgive them for they don't know what they are doing."

What Jesus did on the cross is the epitome of grace. He graced all of humanity when we didn't deserve His grace. He loved when He was wronged. It was truly "amazing grace" that flowed from the cross. When we come to the cross, we also experience that same grace. We have the supernatural ability to love those who have wronged us. We can reach up to Christ and down into our hearts when we stand at the foot of the cross. Then we can pull up the grace of God to love and forgive the people who have wronged us.

If we have wronged someone else, we find forgiveness at the cross. Jesus will forgive us and lead us into complete repentance. At the cross, Christ deals with the root of our sin – "self". There we cry out with the Apostle Paul, "I have been crucified with Christ." We die to self, the old nature. Humility becomes the chief characteristic of our lives when we bow at the cross. Because humility permeates our lives, we are enabled by God's grace to go to those we have wronged and ask forgiveness.

The cross not only reaches upward, but also outward. We can restore broken relationships. But that process begins at the cross. It is not our will power, or cunning schemes of diplomacy, that right wrongs. It's the supernatural grace of God applied to our hearts at the cross.

Victory in interpersonal relationships begins at the cross. Why don't you bow before the cross today and find His grace and victory?

15

RELATING TO GOD BY
REACHING THE WORLD

Occasionally, I'm asked about the timing of revival and evangelism. Does revival take place in our lives and then we become effective witnesses for Christ? Or do we first begin to share our faith in Christ and that results in revival in our lives? The answer to those questions is simply "no" but "yes." Before you become confused, let me explain.

Often a renewing of our faith begins with our understanding that we have become apathetic in our walk with God, or a keen realization that we have not been living the way we ought to live. That's the first step towards revival. We'll never be able to share our faith with others unless we get honest and repent of our sins. God is a holy God, and we can never become intimate in our relationship with Him while there are things in our lives that displease Him.

For example, in Psalms 51, David confessed his sins. After he had become totally honest with God, he asked God to cleanse him and renew him in his walk with God. Only at that moment does he say, "Then I will teach transgressors your ways, and sinners will turn back to you" (Psalms 51:13). David needed to experience a personal revival and then he would be enabled to reach others with the good news of God's love. He understood that he could never be effective in his outreach until he was right in his fellowship with God. Like David, we must first confess our sins, and then we will be able to reach others with the message of Christ.

However, part of our sin can be an unwillingness to share our faith with others. We must also understand that we cannot stay in our "holy huddles" and expect God to send revival. To a certain extent, revival is dependent upon our obedience to the commission of His Son, Jesus. He told us to go into the whole world and tell of the good news of God's love for sinners. How can we walk intimately with Him if we disobey His commands? It's impossible. Often revival begins within us when we begin to reach out and share our faith with others.

Revival has, most often, come on the wings of being broken over our sins or becoming broken over the sins of the world around us. It's not an either/or answer to the question of when renewal takes place within us. David also said in the Psalms, "The sacrifices of God are a broken spirit; a broken and contrite heart, O God, You will not despise" (Psalm 51:17). Revival comes when we are broken before God. It doesn't matter if it's our hearts being broken over our sins or over the sins of a lost world. God's heart is touched by broken hearts. He heals and revives broken hearts. The answer to my original question is a both/and answer. We must deal with the sins in our lives and, at the same time, we need to have a passionate desire to reach the world with the message of Christ. Reaching others is the result of revival in our lives and it's also the reason for revival in our lives. If we are going to have an intimate, victorious walk with Christ, then we must reach out to others with the wonderful message of God's love for sinners.

16

KNOWING THE HEART OF GOD

Close to 100 years ago the great American evangelist, D.L. Moody, was preaching in Lanarkshire, Scotland. A Scottish gentleman from The Brethren Church came to him and said, "I'm coming to America and I would like to visit you there."

Politely, Mr. Moody responded, "Certainly, I would love to see you there." However, he really thought that he would never hear from the gentleman again.

After Moody returned to the United States, he received a letter from the Scot. He wrote, "I'm in New York City, and I'll leave soon for my visit with you in Chicago." Not long afterwards the gentleman showed up in Chicago, prepared to preach. Mr. Moody was speaking somewhere besides his own church. Therefore, out of courtesy, he allowed the gentleman to preach at his church.

When Moody came home that evening he asked his wife, "How did it go at church this evening?"

His wife replied, "It was wonderful, but I don't think you would have liked the message that was delivered." Moody probed further, and his wife told him, "He preached that God loves sinners."

The great evangelist was taken back. "What does he mean?" he asked. "Sinners are under the wrath of God. They're under God's judgment."

Then Mrs. Moody said, "But everything that he said was from the Bible."

The next night Mr. Moody allowed the Scottish brother to preach again, but this time Moody sat listening to him. The man began in Genesis and went through the Bible showing passage after passage that God loves sinners. It was a watershed moment in the life of D. L. Moody. Moody had known the character of God. He rightly knew that God is holy. He understood that nothing unrighteous could stand in God's presence. But Moody had missed the heart of God.

After that encounter with the Scottish preacher, and more importantly, after he came face to face with the heart of God in the Scriptures, Mr. Moody began preaching with a new passion for souls. His eyes were opened to see the love of God for a lost world. He had the words "God is love" placed on one of his buildings. Moody had come to know the heart of God.

I've discovered that many Christians today are just like Mr. Moody was prior to his eye opening experience with the Scottish brother. We often scorn those whose lives are contrary to the nature and character of God. We see people engulfed in their own sins, and we are disgusted. However, we've missed the heart of God. His nature is holiness. We cannot compromise on that. Holiness and sin can't live under the same roof. However, we must also become gripped with the heart of God for a lost and dying world.

Sometimes I travel to regions of the world where the lostness of mankind is so obvious that my heart breaks. When I see multitudes dying in Sub Saharan Africa of AIDS, my heart weeps. Yes, I know that many are dying because of their own sins. The Scriptures are true, "The wages of sin is death." But it's also true that "God so loved the world that He gave His only begotten Son that whosoever would believe on Him would not perish, but have everlasting life." When I see the millions blinded by Hinduism, secularism and Islam, I weep because I know that Christ loves them and He died to forgive them.

When we behold the heart of God, we cannot help but weep for those who have never met the Saviour. It's the heart of God that reaches out to a sinful and rebellious world. It's the heart of God that moved Him to send the Saviour. When we see His heart, we too will weep. We will reach out to those who have never known His love. We will have inscribed on our hearts those words that Mr. Moody had inscribed in one of his buildings, "God is love."

17

I AM NOT ASHAMED

Nearly 2000 years ago, Paul, one of the giants of the Christian faith and author of several books of the New Testament, said, "I am not ashamed of the gospel, because it is the power of God for the salvation of everyone who believes..." (Rom. 1:16). This one time persecutor of Christians had become one of the most vocal and influential voices of Christianity. His conversion was unexplainable, except in terms of the supernatural. But his courage was even more amazing. How could the greatest hater of Christianity become the foremost proponent of the Christian faith?

It certainly wasn't his eloquence of speech and his ability to move the masses that made him so courageous. He said, "My message and my preaching were not with wise and persuasive words, but with a demonstration of the Spirit's power" (1 Cor. 2:4). Paul understood that his conversion was a testimony to the power of God at work in him. God had changed Paul and he never got over that. He knew that only a supernatural work of God in the hearts of others is what produces genuine conversion. Therefore, he was very careful to make sure that his message came in the power of God rather than the power of human ability.

Paul's courage seemed to be rooted in a personal and intimate knowledge of God's power. He could never get over his experience on the road to Damascus. There, he had encountered the resurrected Christ. That experience would thrust him into the world. It would make him willing to die for Jesus. That experience would set a fire burning in his bones that would cause Paul to be a history maker and a world shaker.

Often I hear Christians who grew up in Christian families say, "I don't have a dynamic testimony like Paul. I just can't share my faith with the same enthusiasm and courage that others have." My response to such reasoning is, "You just haven't understood what a dynamic testimony is. The power of a testimony for Christ is not in how bad we've been, but rather in how great God is. It's not how many laws we've broken, how many drugs we've taken, or if we've murdered someone. It took Christ's death, burial and resurrection to save us just as it did Paul. It took the same power and grace of God to forgive a nine year old child as it did to forgive a hater of Christians.

It's not the drama of the conversion that made Paul bold. It was the "power of God unto salvation" that made him courageous. That's also what makes you and me courageous. I tell people everywhere in the world that I preach, "Today is a real miracle day. It's a miracle because I stand here. I wasn't seeking God, but He was seeking me. And one day, He got my attention and changed me. It's a miracle because on a natural level, I wouldn't be here. It's because of God's grace and power that I stand here today."

You don't have to be ashamed. You can be bold and courageous because it took the same power of God to save and forgive you that it did the Apostle Paul. You do have a dynamic testimony if you truly know Christ. That testimony is about what God has done rather than what you've done.

It's His power, His love and His forgiveness that makes us courageous. You can say with as much conviction as Paul said, "I am not ashamed."

18

MY POSITION IN CHRIST

Several years ago a little lady who had been a missionary for many years was visiting a pastor in a city in the United States that had many street gangs. It was a dangerous place to live and minister. Consequently, the pastor was taking a karate course to learn how to defend himself. When the little missionary lady discovered what the pastor was doing, she was shocked.

"Why are you taking karate lessons?" she quickly asked.

The pastor sheepishly responded, "You must understand that it's very dangerous here. I need to be able to protect myself."

"Then you don't understand your position in Christ."

"What do you mean?" the pastor asked.

The little missionary then began to explain a great theological and practical truth about victory in Christ. She began drawing circles. After the first circle she said, "This circle represents your life." She then drew a bigger circle around the first one. "The bigger circle represents Christ. The Bible says that you are in Christ. Do you understand?" she questioned.

After a positive response, the little lady then drew an even bigger circle around the first two circles. "That circle" she said, "represents the Father. You are in Christ and Christ is in the Father." Then she drew a small circle inside the first circle. "That circle represents the Holy Spirit who lives inside you. You are in Christ. Christ is in the Father. And the Holy Spirit lives in you."

After the pastor agreed, the little missionary lady continued, "Before the devil can do anything to harm you, he has to first go through the Father and get permission from Him. If the Father gives him permission to attack you, he then must go through the Son. If the Son gives him permission to attack you, then you have the blessed Holy Spirit living within you. And the Bible says that 'greater is He who lives in you than he who lives in the world.' Then why are you so afraid? The safest place in the world to be is 'in Christ'."

That little lady understood a great truth about victorious Christian living. Our victory is completely related to our position in Christ. Therefore, every day we need to awaken and clothe ourselves with Christ. We need to take time to recognize that we are in Christ. By faith, we must claim Christ's protection over us. We need to ask the Holy Spirit to take complete control of our lives. As He fills us, we will experience victory over the attacks that Satan has against us.

Perhaps it would do us good to draw a few circles and remind ourselves of our position in Christ. I've walked into a revolution, the aftermath of an attempted genocide, been in airports that terrorists were threatening to blow up, had knives put to my throat, and been shot at as I've attempted to bring the message of God's love around the world. But I've learned that the safest place in the world is "in Christ." I need to simply take time daily to place myself in Christ and allow Christ to fill me. There's no safer place in the world than "abiding in Christ."

19

THE SURRENDERED LIFE

A friend of mine once asked a Christian leader from Romania why the church in the Western world had lost its power with God and with man. The Romanian Christian leader answered with what I believe is one of the great root problems within the church. He firmly stated, "The church has substituted commitment for surrender." He was right. There are many hard working and committed Christians in the church today, but few surrendered ones.

There's a great difference in the surrendered life and the committed life. The committed life emphasizes what we must do for Christ. The surrendered says we can do nothing. The committed life communicates my accomplishments, but the surrendered life clearly calls for God's power. The committed life is that of a hard worker, but the surrendered life is that of a slave.

Surrender to Christ basically means that we have lost our will to His will. We have no rights. We have signed our life over to Him. We will go where He wants us to go and do what He wants us to do. We will speak what He wants us to speak and be what He wants us to be. The surrendered life is admitting that Christ has won the victory over our will. It's allowing Him to accomplish His work in and through us. It's praying as Jesus prayed, "Not my will, but Thine be done."

I was once ministering with a group of young people in

East Germany. At that time in the history of that nation, it was very dangerous to meet with me. At the close of the meeting, one of them came to me and said, "I came to know Christ some time ago. However, I have lost the joy of what Christ has done in my heart." We prayed together, and I will never forget the prayer of that young person.

"Take control of my life, dear God," she prayed, "no matter what the cost." After I finished praying with that young lady, I looked around and all of the young people were on their knees praying. Every one of them had the same phrase at the end of their prayer. One prayed, "I surrender to you, God, no matter what the cost." Each one of them counted the cost and surrendered fully to God. It was a touching moment.

I've often heard Christians commit themselves to God in prayer. But what I heard from those East German young people was much more than commitment. It was absolute surrender to the will of God. They were willing for God to take control of their lives no matter what the cost. It did cost them. It cost them their educational opportunities – their future. But they had becomes slaves of Jesus. Interestingly, this slavery is what made them victorious in their lives.

I once asked Dr. Bill Bright, founder of Campus Crusade For Christ, if there was ever a watershed moment in his Christian life that propelled him into the work that God has given him. He told me, "Years ago, Vonette and I made a decision to become slaves of Jesus Christ. That decision set the course of my entire Christian life and ministry."

It's only as we become slaves of Jesus that we experience His victory. It's only as we lose our will to His will that we find joy in life. It's only as we die to our abilities that we can appropriate His supernatural abilities. It's only as we are surrendered to Him that we know His supernatural ability. It's what the old hymn writer said, "All to Jesus, I surrender. All to Him I freely give." That's when victory begins.

20

THE CRUCIFIED LIFE

My heart burned with the love of Christ during the first three years of my Christian life. I wanted to tell everyone of His great love. I couldn't wait to come into His presence through prayer and reading the Bible. Those were wonderful days that I shall never forget. There was a special place where I would meet with Him in the mornings. The memories of those days linger with me 34 years later.

After three years something happened in my Christian experience. The flame of the love of God began to die down in my heart. I didn't know what to do. I knew that I was a Christian, but I no longer experienced the victory that I once knew. I didn't know how to recapture that flame that once burned deep within my soul.

One day, I met a man named Leo Humphrey. He was a red headed ball of fire. He witnessed to everyone that he met. When I saw the fire of God's love burning deep within him, I realized how defeated I really was in my Christian life. One night Leo and I were ministering together in a beach side community on the Gulf of Mexico. I confided in Leo, "I'm defeated. I don't know what to do. I struggle in my walk with God."

That night Leo and I prayed together. I thought it was for about a half an hour. However, I was surprised to see the sun rising the next morning. We had prayed through the night. That night was a turning point in my personal walk with God.

That night I took my wife and placed her in a casket. I took my furniture and placed it in a casket. I took my automobile, my clothes, and all of my material possessions and placed them in that casket. I took my ambition to be some well known preacher and placed it in that casket. I took my future dreams and aspirations and placed them in that casket. Then I crawled into the casket and I died.

By now, you may be wondering what in the world I'm talking about. No, I didn't physically do that. But I did spiritually. Sammy Tippit died. I died to the "self life" – to ego, pride, self-sufficiency, and selfishness. The Apostle Paul said, "I have been crucified with Christ; nevertheless, I live. Yet not I, but Christ lives in me. And the life I now live in the flesh, I live by the faith of the Son of God" (Gal. 2:20). Paul had not been physically crucified with Christ, but he had died spiritually to the "self life." His life could only be described by "Christ who lived in him."

When I discovered this great truth, the fire of God's love began to burn deep within my soul once again. Actually, I had died to self when I became a Christian. The "old man" had died and I was raised to a new life in Christ. That's why I had experienced so much victory in the beginning of my Christian life. But somewhere along the way, I thought that I could live the Christian life. I tried, and I failed miserably.

The victorious Christian life is the crucified life. It's the life that has died to self and has been raised to victory by the indwelling presence of Jesus Christ. It's the life that truly understands, "no longer I, but Christ who lives in me." It's dead to self and alive in Christ.

I had to climb in a casket one evening. Only then did I begin to experience the victorious Christian life. There's a casket waiting for each one of us. Life results from death. We'll never know the resurrected power of Christ until we've experienced the crucified life with Him.

21

DYING DAILY

"I die every day!" The great scholars of history may not understand those words, but they are clearly understood by every victorious Christian. The secret to the victorious Christian life is found in those words penned by the Apostle Paul nearly 2000 years ago. He not only wrote of this death to the believers in Corinth but also to the followers of Christ in Galatia and Rome. Paul understood that the victorious life was the fruit of the crucified life.

But exactly what did he mean when he wrote in 1 Corinthians 15:31, "I die every day"? Paul was speaking about a spiritual reality that many Christians have failed to grasp. This truth is the key that unlocks the door of Victorious Christian Living. It's the foundation upon which victory is built in our lives. It's the element which gives every believer victory over the areas of our lives where we seem to struggle endlessly. Out of the death of Christ came the greatest victory known to mankind – the resurrected life of Christ.

When we come to know Christ, there is something deeply spiritual that transpires in our lives. Our old life dies and we receive a new life. That's why Paul wrote, "Therefore, if anyone is in Christ, he is a new creation; the old has gone, the new has come" (2 Cor. 5:17). Our lives are eternally and practically transformed at the moment we trust Christ as our Lord and Saviour.

I once met a group of young people from the Philippines

that had come to know Christ. They were travelling throughout Europe singing and ministering. One of their songs touched my heart because in its simplicity it gave my testimony and the testimony of every true follower of Christ. "I'll never be the same again, oh no. I'll never be the same again, oh no. Since I met the Lord, I am not the same and I'll never be the same again." When Christ comes into our lives, we will never be the same again because our old life has died and we now have a new life dwelling deep within – the life of Christ through the Holy Spirit.

Then why do we experience defeat? It's simply because we try to live in our own power. We must learn to die daily. As we take our position as dead to self, then the Holy Spirit manifests the life of Christ within us. We bear the fruit of the life of Christ. Just as Christ had to die in order to be resurrected, we must die daily to self in order to experience the resurrected life of Christ.

Quite frankly, I must admit to you that the days in which I wake up and attempt to live the Christian life on my own, I fail miserably. But on the days that I wake up and say to God, "I can't live the Christian life today. So, I die today. I die to my ambitions and desires. I die to my abilities and efforts. I die to my self centeredness," then on those days I experience victory. I discover the truth of which Paul wrote, "it's no longer I who lives, but Christ who lives in me" (Gal. 2:20b).

A friend of mine many years ago told me that he was contemplating suicide. He sat in his church pew weeping. His pastor saw him and asked, "Why are you crying?" My friend replied, "I don't want to live any more. I want to die." The pastor shocked my friend when he said, "Okay, go ahead. Die."

My friend looked up at the pastor and said, "Wha, what do you mean?" The godly pastor then opened the Scriptures to this young man to the great truth of dying to self so that Christ can live within us. My friend died that day. Today he's a minister of the gospel of Christ. God is using his life wonderfully. He learned the secret to the victorious Christian life. He learned to die – die every day.

22

FILLED WITH THE SPIRIT

The victorious Christian life stands in stark contrast with the typical Christian life. It's one of dependence upon God rather than independence from Him. It's a life of trusting in Him rather than trying in our own power. It's being emptied of self and filled with God's Spirit. We're no longer in control of our lives, but Christ is holding the reins of our hearts.

God commands His children to be filled with the Spirit (Eph. 5:18). Yet, few know what it means to live in the fullness of His Spirit. There's much talk about being filled with the Holy Spirit but very little walk in the power of the Spirit. The Spirit-filled life is one of total abandonment to God.

Dr. Bill Bright, president and founder of Campus Crusade For Christ, describes being filled with the Holy Spirit as spiritual breathing. "As we confess our sins," he says, "we are exhaling." God cleanses us from sin and we take our position as dead to self. But then Dr. Bright says that the believer must "inhale." We must appropriate the fullness of the Spirit by faith.

Control is the key to the fullness of the Holy Spirit in our lives. It means that Christ is in control of our lives when we are filled with the Spirit. He directs our paths and empowers us to be all that God intended. That's why the victorious Christian life is one under the control of the

Spirit. A life under the control of the Holy Spirit will always produce fruit that's pleasing to God.

I came across this principle of being filled with the Holy Spirit as a new believer. I studied at Campus Crusade For Christ for two weeks not long after I came to know Christ. I heard Dr. Bright teach this great truth of spiritual breathing. He challenged us to get alone and take a piece of paper and write our known sins. He then said, "After you've written them all on the paper, then pray this prayer, 'Lord, search my heart and show me if there's anything displeasing to you.' If He shows you anything else, then write it down. Agree with God that it's wrong and turn from it. He will forgive and cleanse you. Then ask God to fill you with the Holy Spirit."

I took Dr. Bright up on his challenge. When I found a quiet spot where I could be alone with God, I wrote out all of my known sins. I then prayed and asked God to show me anything in my life that displeased Him. Do you know what happened? I had to get more paper. God showed me so much that I had called "weaknesses" or "problems." God showed me that it was sin. As I confessed those things and turned from them, He cleansed me.

I then asked God to fill me with His Spirit. I didn't have an earth-shattering experience. I didn't see any visions or speak in any unknown tongues. I just allowed Him by faith to have complete control of every area of my life. There was no great sensation to prove that I had been filled with the Spirit. But as I have learned to do that daily, the evidence has shown up in my life. As I allow the Holy Spirit to have control of my life, He produces the fruit of His righteousness within me. It works its way out of my heart and is manifested as love, joy, peace, patience, kindness, goodness, faithfulness, gentleness and self-control. In other words the Spirit-filled life is one of choosing daily to allow the Holy Spirit to be in control rather than self.

The choice is yours. It's victory or defeat; His power or your weakness; the fruit of the Spirit or the deeds of the flesh; Christ in control or self at the centre. It's your choice to make. The apostle years ago under the inspiration of the Holy Spirit penned these words, "be filled with the Holy Spirit" (Eph. 5:18). If you have been emptied of sin and self, you're in a position to be filled with the Spirit. Why don't you ask God to do that in your life right now?

23

WALKING IN THE SPIRIT

Someone has said, "What's important in the Christian life is not how high you can jump, but how straight you can walk once you've landed." That's certainly true in relationship to the fullness of the Holy Spirit. I hear many people debating what it means to be filled with the Holy Spirit today. There are good and faithful people on both sides of the issue. But sometimes I think that we've missed the whole reason that God told us to be filled with the Holy Spirit. It wasn't so we could debate about how high we need to jump, but rather to learn how to walk straight in a crooked world.

The Apostle Paul wrote to the church at Galatia about what it meant to be filled with the Holy Spirit. He characterized the life filled with the Holy Spirit as he wrote of the fruit of the Spirit. He then says in Gal. 5:16, "But I say to you, walk by the Spirit and you will not carry out the desire of the flesh." He then re-emphasizes this great need by saying, "If we live by the Spirit, let us also walk by the Spirit" (Gal. 5:25). He knew that it was more important how we walked than how we talked. There was a great need not only to talk about the power of the Holy Spirit, but to live out a life under the control of the Holy Spirit.

It's been my experience that Christians today are much better at talking about the fullness of the Holy Spirit than we are at walking daily in the power of the Holy Spirit. We must learn to walk by the Spirit. It's interesting that when Paul wrote to the church in Ephesus, he contrasted being filled with the Holy Spirit with getting drunk. I'm not proud of the fact that before I became a Christian, I had been drunk on several occasions. One of the first things that happened when I drank too much was that it affected the manner in which I walked. I couldn't walk straight no matter how hard I tried.

There's a contrasting truth when we are filled with the Holy Spirit. We walk straight spiritually, and there's no effort. We're no longer living in our own power. We're walking under the influence of the Holy Spirit. The only way He walks is the straight and narrow way. He walks the way of holiness and purity. He walks the road of integrity. When we are controlled by the Holy Spirit, then we, too, will walk in the way of holiness, purity, and integrity.

There are many who begin well in the Christian life, but do not finish well. Often it's because they have not learned to draw from the living waters deep within themselves. We must daily appropriate the fullness of the Holy Spirit in our lives. He is our enabler. He empowers us to live the way we ought to live. He overcomes every weakness and obstacle in our walk with God. He is our source of victory. He is the one who will see us through to the end. He enables us to complete that which was begun in us.

We are absolutely dependent upon the Holy Spirit for all of our strength in the Christian life. Therefore, we must depend upon Him as we walk daily. We will then supernaturally naturally walk in purity and holiness of life.

Today, I ask you this question. No, it's not how high you've jumped spiritually. It's how straight have you been walking? The answer to that question speaks volumes of how much you truly know about the fullness of the Holy Spirit.

24

WORKING IN THE SPIRIT

Moses was a man mightily used of God. But there was one great lesson that he had to learn before God could make his life a great instrument in His hands. He needed to know that the work of God had to be done in the power of God. Moses had to go to school in the Midianite desert in order to learn that great lesson – God's work must be done in the power of God's Spirit and not the power of the human flesh.

When Moses was in Egypt during the first forty years of his life, he was young and powerful. He grew up as the son of the Pharaoh's daughter. He tried to do the right thing in helping his Hebrew brethren, but he failed miserably. When he saw an Egyptian mistreating his Hebrew kinsman, he killed him and hid him in the sand. However, his actions only brought more sufferings to his people. He fled to the Midianite desert. There he learned to work in the power of God's Spirit.

After his encounter with God on the mountain, he would never be the same. He went back to Egypt and was God's instrument to bring freedom to his people. But he didn't return in the power of his own strength. He came back to Egypt in the authority and might of God's Spirit. It was only then that he became a useful instrument in the hands of a mighty God. It was only when he had learned to work in the power of God's Spirit that he was enabled to be all that God wanted him to be.

When I first became a Christian I had the opportunity to hear Dr. Billy Graham. I had heard that he was being used as God's man for this generation. I travelled to Houston, Texas to listen to Dr. Graham speak in the huge indoor stadium, the Astrodome. As I listened to him speak, I must admit I thought to myself, "What's so special about this guy? He's a decent speaker, but he's not that great." I had been trained in public oratory, and I didn't see anything special about Dr. Graham.

When he came to the invitation for people to come to Christ, I remember praying, "Oh, God, help him not to feel too bad if no one comes forward to accept Christ." Was I ever surprised! Thousands of people went to the front of the platform to pray with Dr. Graham. I'm ashamed to admit what I thought next. I thought if thousands of people were coming to Christ through a somewhat better than average speaker, then the whole world would turn to Christ when they heard me speak!

I was in for a second great surprise! Not long after that I had the opportunity to preach an evangelistic meeting myself. I used all of the oratory skills that I could possibly muster. I had an intriguing introduction, a solid body of thoughts, and a very dramatic conclusion. I used all of the right voice inflections and made gestures at the right moment. When I gave the invitation, do you know what happened? Nothing!

You see, there was something that I didn't know that Dr. Graham knew. The work of God must be done in the power of the Holy Spirit and not the power of the human flesh. It's not our abilities, but His abilities, that will get the job done. Our responsibility is to be available to Him. He will use us if we are available. Just as Moses had to learn that the work of God had to be done in the power of the Holy Spirit, I, too, had to learn this great lesson.

Many of us want to work for God. If we are to be effective in the kingdom of God, then we must learn to work in the power of the Spirit of God. Our walk in the Spirit enables us to live victoriously. Our work in the Spirit enables us to accomplish His will. The end result is joy in seeing His will accomplished through our works and His enablement. What God said to the prophet of old is still true today – it's "not by might, nor by power, but by My Spirit."

25

WORSHIPPING IN THE SPIRIT

If you were to die right now, do you have the confidence that you have done what you were created to do with your life? When my life comes to an end, I want to know that I did with my life what God created me to do. That's truly a victorious Christian life. The key to doing that is in understanding your purpose in life. Purpose isn't derived from our great achievements or in how much wealth or influence we've acquired. God's not going to ask us about our financial holdings when we get to heaven. He's not going to want to know how much influence, power, or possessions we accrued. All of those things will be meaningless when our lives draw to a conclusion.

So, what is the real purpose of life? God created us to know, love, and worship Him. I believe that deep in the heart of every man, woman, boy, and girl on this planet is a deep innate desire to worship the God who created them. That's why there are so many religions in the world. That's why religion immediately began to flourish in former communist countries as soon as freedom came to those countries. Even though the people had been taught all of their lives that there is no God, something deep within them cried out to know and worship the true and living God. Man was created with a profound longing to worship God.

But that brings us to a second question – what is true worship? If there are so many religions and beliefs, then which one is right? It's impossible for all of them to be right because they often contradict one another. Hindus worship a multiplicity of gods while Muslims worship only one God. Jews worship one God also, but Judaism and Islam stand in total opposition to each other. Who's right? Where do the true worshippers worship? That same question was asked of Jesus nearly 2000 years ago.

A Samaritan woman asked Jesus about the location of the true worshippers. Jesus said something that should cause every person on this planet to do a lot of introspection. He said that "a time is coming and has now come when the true worshippers will worship the Father in spirit and truth, for they are the kind of worshippers the Father seeks" (John 4:23 NIV). The truth is that Jesus is the Son of the living God – the most unique human being to ever grace this planet. He was all God and yet all man. He was given the name "Emmanuel" which means "God with us." Worshipping in truth is the worship of Jesus, the Christ.

But what does it mean to worship in spirit? In the chapter preceding the story of the Samaritan woman, Jesus told one of the most religious men in all of Israel that he or anyone else must be born of the Spirit if he is to enter the kingdom of heaven. Before we can worship in spirit, we must then be born of the Spirit of God. Religion is the expression of man attempting to appease God with external rituals. But true worship is the deep worship that is a result of one's faith in Christ which produces a spiritual birth in our lives.

When Christ came into my heart, I no longer just went through the outward form of religion. I began to worship from the deepest part of my being. I began to worship in Spirit. The greatest joy in my life has resulted from those times of deep intimate worship of Jesus Christ. Victorious and joyful Christian living comes from worshipping the Saviour from the deepest parts of our hearts.

If you want to experience victory in your life, then begin to do what you were created to do. Find a time and a place and worship Jesus. You'll be amazed at how much your perspective in life will change when you have been doing what God created you to do.

26

THE JOYFUL CHRISTIAN LIFE

For many years I had a misconception of what it meant to be a Christian. I thought a Christian was someone who was always very sombre with a harsh outlook on life. Somehow, I never imagined that the Christian life could be a joyful one. Of course, I also had a misconception about what joy really is. I thought joy was induced from outside of my own self. As someone who had no personal relationship with Christ, I based my joy on external circumstances and other people.

When Christ came into my heart, I made a wonderful discovery – Christianity isn't some weird form of drudgery whereby I must do things that I really don't enjoy doing. In fact I learned that the opposite is true. When Christ lives in a person's heart, there's joy unspeakable that fills his life. Christian joy isn't dependant upon outward circumstances or other people. It comes from the deep indwelling presence of the Holy Spirit. In fact, the first two evidences of the Holy Spirit working in the life of the believer are love and joy.

There are three aspects of joy about which the Bible speaks: 1) a mental and emotional state of being; 2) a fruit of the Holy Spirit indwelling the believer; and 3) a sense of moral satisfaction. Before I came to know Christ personally, one of my favourite popular songs had a line that went like this, "I can't get no satisfaction." That line was repeated over and over in the song. Those lyrics described my life. However, after I became a Christian,

God put a new song in my heart, "I've found satisfaction." That's true joy! It's the satisfaction of knowing in the deepest part of your being that you have found the real purpose of life – that you're doing what you were created to do with your life.

But joy is much more than a moral satisfaction. It's an emotional and psychological state of mind. Joy is not produced from without, but from within. Christian joy isn't dependent upon our acceptance or rejection by people. We've been accepted by God because of what Christ did on the cross 2000 years ago. That produces an internal and eternal joy that is unspeakable and indescribable. The Christian doesn't need a party or a person to establish joy in his life. His emotional and psychological state of mind is produced by his acceptance by Christ.

But joy in the life of the Christian is primarily a quality produced by the indwelling Holy Spirit. Paul wrote to the Christians in Galatia, "But the fruit of the Spirit is love, joy, peace…."(Gal. 5:22 NIV). It is a supernatural natural work of grace in the life of the believer. As we yield our lives to the control of the Holy Spirit, He supernaturally produces joy in our hearts. This joy goes far beyond the circumstances of the day. It transcends the negativism that people attempt to dump on us. It's the joy of the Lord who is in us.

The victorious Christian life is a joyful one. Our joy is not rooted in the circumstances of life nor the approval of men. It's a joy that rises from deep within. It's a mental, moral, and psychological state that's produced by the deep work of Christ on the cross and the Holy Spirit who dwells within our hearts and minds. The joy of the Lord is our strength.

27

PEACE THAT PASSES UNDERSTANDING

I was quite intrigued the first time I visited Romania. I found the people to be some of the most hospitable in the world. But there was one custom among the Christians that really stirred my curiosity. They greeted one another with the word, "Pace." It's pronounced pach-ey and simply means "peace." The reason their greeting intrigued me was because when I first travelled into the country there was no real external peace, especially among Christians.

Christians were hunted, persecuted, lost their jobs, and often placed in prison. So, why did these believers greet each other with the word "peace"? The non-Christian community certainly didn't greet each other in that way. What was it that caused these outcasts of society to say "peace" when they saw one another? It didn't make sense.

However, after I came to know many of these dear brothers and sisters, I began to understand. They were enemies of the communist regime but friends with God. They had an intimate walk with the Lord that produced what the Apostle Paul said was a peace that passed all understanding. It doesn't make sense to have peace in the middle of extreme trials and difficulties. But that's what God specializes in. He has a way of making sense out of nonsense.

Peace is a by-product of the victorious Christian life. It's a fruit of the Holy Spirit that's produced in the believer who is fully yielded to Christ and trusting in Him. The Old

Testament speaks of peace as an outward sense, it often had a physical meaning. However, the emphasis of peace in the New Testament was directly related to the innermost part of our lives and our relationship with God.

We have peace with God because of what Jesus did on the cross. Paul wrote, "Therefore, since we have been justified through faith, we have peace with God through our Lord Jesus Christ" (Rom. 5:1 NIV). I ceased the war with God when I placed my faith in Christ. I'll never forget that night. I walked out of the church where I prayed to receive Christ with peace flowing in my heart. It was like a thousand pounds were lifted from my shoulders. I was at peace with the God who created me.

The wonderful thing about the Christian life is that we can also know the peace of God. We can be at peace with God, but also experience the peace of God. The Christian is not exempt from trials and difficulties in his life. But he can be exempt from the turmoil of the heart that often accompanies those tribulations. That's why Paul also wrote, "Do not be anxious about anything, but in everything, by prayer and petition, with thanksgiving, present your requests to God, and the peace of God, which transcends all understanding, will guard your hearts and your minds in Christ Jesus" (Phil. 4:6, 7 NIV).

No, it doesn't make sense to have peace in the midst of tragedy and pain. It's impossible to understand why we experience all of the problems that we face. But the victorious Christian life is one that produces peace in the midst of pain; joy in times of suffering; and love when we're hated. Only the indwelling Christ can produce such a life. He is able because He is the Prince of Peace.

Peace is a word with several different meanings in the Old and New Testaments.

The Old Testament meaning of peace was completeness, soundness, and well-being of the total person. This peace was considered God-given, obtained by following the Law (Ps. 119:165). Peace sometimes had a physical meaning, suggesting security (Ps. 4:8), contentment (Is. 26:3), prosperity (Ps. 122:6-7) and the absence of war (1 Sam. 7:14). The traditional Jewish greeting *shalom* was a wish for peace.

In the New Testament, peace often refers to the inner tranquillity and poise of the Christian whose trust is in God through Christ. This understanding was originally expressed in the Old Testament writings about the coming MESSIAH (Is. 9:6-7). The peace that Jesus Christ spoke of was a combination of hope, trust, and quiet in the mind and soul, brought about by a reconciliation with God. Such peace was proclaimed by the host of angels at Christ's birth (Luke 2:14), and by Christ Himself in His SERMON ON THE MOUNT (Matt. 5:9) and during His ministry. He also taught about this kind of peace at the Lord's Supper, shortly before His death (John 14:27).

The apostle Paul later wrote that such peace and spiritual blessedness was a direct result of faith in Christ (Rom. 5:1).[1]

Therefore, since we have been justified through faith, we have peace with God through our Lord Jesus Christ, (Rom. 5:1 NIV)

---

1. from Nelson's Illustrated Bible Dictionary

Do not be anxious about anything, but in everything, by prayer and petition, with thanksgiving, present your requests to God. (Phil. 4:6 NIV)

And the peace of God, which transcends all understanding, will guard your hearts and your minds in Christ Jesus. (Phil. 4:7 NIV)

28

VICTORY OVER TEMPTATION

Many Christians find themselves exasperated because of overwhelming defeat from temptation. Many Christians doubt whether victory over temptation could ever be achieved. In desperation they've given up. However, this need not be. God has made provision for our victory over any and every temptation. We do not have to limp to the finish line of life bruised, battered, and defeated. We can run the race of life with our eyes fixed on the Saviour who always leads us into His triumph.

God has given us an example and the power to be overcomers. The genuine follower of Christ will always face temptation. It's always been a part of life, dating back all the way to the Garden of Eden. Adam was tempted. Noah, Abraham, Moses, Peter, Paul and John have all faced temptation. It's impossible to go through life without temptation. However, the Bible says that with every temptation, God has provided a way of escape.

There's one great example in the Scriptures where we see absolute victory over temptation. Jesus was tempted in every manner in which you and I have been tempted. There are three fundamental areas in which Satan tempts the believer – 1) the lust of the flesh; 2) the lust of the eyes; and 3) the boastful pride of life. It's recorded in Matthew (chapter 4 verses 1-11) that Jesus was tempted in all three of these areas. He was first tempted with the lust of the flesh. Satan enticed Him to turn a stone into bread (he appealed to the lust of the flesh). He then attempted to lure Jesus into a prideful attitude about who He is. Satan reasoned that if Jesus was the Son of God, then He could cast Himself off the pinnacle of the temple and nothing would happen. That was the epitome of the boastful pride of life. Finally, Jesus was tempted with the lust of the eyes. He was shown and offered the kingdoms of the world.

But Jesus refused to yield to the temptations of Satan. He overcame the snares of the evil one. Therefore, Jesus offers us an example and the Source to overcome temptation. First, Jesus offers us an example. In each instance, Jesus countered the temptation with the Word of God. When Satan lured Him, Jesus stood upon the Scriptures. He quoted the Bible. He obeyed the Bible. The Bible was a mighty sword in the hands of the Son of Man. With it, He tore down every rationalization that the enemy would throw His way. When Satan then tried to deceive Jesus by also quoting Scripture (out of its proper context), Jesus simply quoted Scripture in its proper context. Jesus is our example of how to overcome temptation. We have the same weapon that Jesus used to overcome temptation.

But as we look at the temptation of Jesus in its proper context, we also find the Source of our victory. Immediately before Jesus was tempted, He had been baptized. During that time the Holy Spirit descended upon Him as a dove. The earthly ministry of Jesus did not begin until after He had publicly positioned Himself in obedience through His baptism and after the anointing of the Holy Spirit came upon His life. It was this empowering of the Holy Spirit that was the secret to the victory of Jesus.

Although Jesus was, is, and always will be God, He left

His throne of glory and took upon Himself the clothes of humanity. He lived as we lived. He walked and struggled just as we do. Yet, He was without sin. As a man, He was completely dependent upon the Holy Spirit. Jesus was empowered by the Holy Spirit just as we must be empowered by the Holy Spirit in order to experience victory. Overcoming temptation is a matter of yielding to and abiding in the Holy Spirit. That's our source of victory. Jesus is our example and the Holy Spirit is our resource. As we look unto Jesus, we emerge from temptation as "more than conquerors."

29

VICTORY OVER ANGER

Is it okay to be angry or not? Quite often I find that Christians are confused over the subject of anger. "The Bible tells us to be angry but not to sin," I frequently hear Christians say in defence of one of their outbursts. However, the kind of rage many people today experience isn't the kind of anger that the Bible is talking about when it says that we're not to let the sun go down on our anger.

So, when is anger good and when is it bad? First, we need to understand anger from a Biblical perspective. There are three Greek words used in the New Testament that are translated as the verb anger: 1) The first is the word *thumos* which is an agitated feeling which results in outbursts; the next word is *parorgismos* which is a more thoughtful feeling or "righteous indignation" – a disgust for injustice; the final word is *aganaktesis* which refers to physical pain or irritation.

It is this first word *thumos* that I want to deal with when I speak of victory over anger. It's this word that is used in Galatians 5:20 when describing the deeds of the flesh. The King James Version of the Bible translates it as wrath. No matter what the translation, there's one thing that is not arguable – *thumoi* in Galatians 5:20 is a work of the flesh and not pleasing to God. We must overcome those feelings. There's no excuse for the Christian to have outbursts of *thumoi* (anger). We cannot wrap our anger with spiritual terminology and parade it as something holy. It's a product of a life lived in the power of the flesh and not the Spirit. It's abominable to God.

Let's call this kind of outburst of anger what it is – sin. A husband yelling at a wife in the name of the Lord is sin. A husband or wife beating a child from an outburst of anger is sin. Christians having outbursts of anger in the work of God is inexcusable. We must recognize the deeds of the flesh and deal with them accordingly.

How then do we overcome anger? If we look closely at the cause of much of our anger, we will normally find that it's a result of deep hurt. We become angry because we feel mistreated or that we have received a raw deal in life. Or perhaps it's because someone has inflicted pain and injury upon us. Therefore, we hold unresolved feelings of bitterness that eventually make their way out of our lives in outbursts of anger. We do and say things that are not in sync with how we would normally respond to people and situations.

There's one story in the Bible that has been a tremendous help to me in overcoming feelings that have been harboured in my heart. Joseph had been treated unjustly by his brothers. If anyone had a reason to become angry, Joseph did. Yet, when he saw his brothers later in life, he responded to them saying, "You meant it for evil, but God meant it for good." Joseph understood this great truth. God had a very specific plan for his life. Even though he had received what could have easily been perceived as a "raw deal" in life, he looked beyond his circumstances. He saw God's hand and God's provision.

Consequently, he didn't become bitter. There were no outbursts of *thumoi*. There was an unbelievable sense of calm, love, and peace that filled his heart.

Joseph knew that God is sovereign. He trusted in His reign and rule in His life. I believe that we can overcome those horrible outbursts of anger that plague our lives. We, too, must trust in God as our sovereign Lord. We need to get our focus off our circumstances and onto His omnipotence. We need to see that He is in control. That will only come as we spend time with Him in His Word and in prayer. Self-control is a fruit of the Spirit. As I spend time in the fullness of His presence, I am at peace. When stormy circumstances engulf my life, I don't have to give in to outbursts of anger. I can rest in sweet assurance and peace that God is in control. That gives me victory over anger.

30

VICTORY OVER LUST

The victorious Christian life is one that can be produced only by God working in and through us. Our victory doesn't lie in our great abilities, but rather in our availability to God and His power. He's capable of giving us victory over any and every besetting sin in our lives. He is our source. He's our strength. He's the rock upon which we can stand when temptations flood our souls. But there's one question that plagues our hearts and minds. If God is able to deliver us, then why do we find ourselves yielding to those sins that trouble us?

That question is especially difficult to answer in relation to the lusts of the heart. Sadly, many Christian leaders have found themselves defeated in this area of their lives. Some have lost their families. Others harbour lusts in places of their hearts where no one would ever suspect. I've had more than one person ask me if it's really possible to have victory over the lusts of the heart.

The good news is that Jesus has been tempted in every manner in which we have been tempted. Yet, He was without sin. As we trust completely in Him, we can experience victory – His victory. There are two distinct characteristics of the life that experiences victory over lust. One is deeply spiritual. The other is very practical. Lust begins in the heart, but is consummated with physical actions. If we are to know victory over lust then we must deal with both areas of our lives.

The Bible describes David as a man after God's own heart. He loved God and trusted in Him alone. However, David yielded to the lusts of the heart in the latter part of his life and became defeated. His lust led to adultery and even murder. The sins and crimes of David were conceived in his heart on a roof one evening. He saw a beautiful woman named Bathsheba. She was bathing. That was a critical moment. David had a decision to make. Would he continue to look and allow lust to grow in his heart, or would he immediately turn and walk away from the temptation? Unfortunately, David made the wrong decision.

We can learn much from David's failure. First, it doesn't matter how many victories that you've experienced in your walk with God. You'll still have to choose against the lusts of the heart all of your life. A well known theology professor once told me that he was speaking to an elderly Christian gentleman of about 80 years of age. He asked the saintly man, "How old is a person when he no longer has to deal with lust?" The old man thoughtfully replied, "I really don't know. But I do know this. It's definitely after 80 years of age." As long as we're clothed in this old flesh, we'll have to deal with lust.

Second, victory or defeat begins with heart decisions. David could have immediately turned away from the privacy of the woman bathing. But he didn't. He allowed himself to look and continue to look until lust was finally conceived. His sin began before he ever committed adultery. It began in his heart. That's why Jesus pointed to the lust of the heart being the root of adultery.

Finally, David acted upon his lust. First, he sent someone to find out about the woman. Then he sent for her and committed adultery. Finally, he hatched a plan to have her husband killed. What began with an innocent look ended in the death of one of David's soldiers. At any point, he could have stopped his sin. But he continued in it until the deeds of death had grown from the tree of transgression.

If we are to know victory over lust, then we must go back to the conception of the sin. We must learn to deal with sin where it was initiated in our hearts. We must learn to make wise decisions. The choices that we make will ultimately result in life or death. We must learn to choose Jesus.

31

VICTORY OVER JEALOUSY

There are some feelings of the soul that are so deep that we often wonder why we were created the way we are. Jealousy is one of those feelings that lurks in the dark recesses of our hearts and seems to come out at the most opportune time. Jealousy has its roots in insecurity. It's basically derived from the fear of loss. A man becomes obsessively jealous because he's afraid he'll lose his wife or girlfriend. One worker is jealous of another one because he or she is afraid that he may lose his position or esteem. Jealousy is rooted in fear and fear is based in insecurity.

There's only one cure for the deep wounds of the soul – faith in Jesus. Faith is the opposite of fear, and Jesus is the source of security. It's only through our trust in Him that we find victory over the fruit of our insecurity. Jesus is our Victor. He was the most secure man to ever grace this planet. He is our Rock, our Shield, and our Defender. He is the secure place during the storms that rage about us. It's only as we come to Him in simple childlike faith that we find peace in the storms.

When Christ came into my life, God set me free from many things. I no longer was a slave to alcohol, sex, and ego. The truth of God's love had set me free. However, I still struggled with jealousy for a long time. I tried to overcome the jealousy, but found it impossible. It seemed as though the harder I tried, the more jealous I became. So,

I just gritted my teeth and tried even more not to be jealous. But jealousy had me trapped in a world of insecurity.

One day someone shared with me the secret of victory in the Christian life. It was not in what I could do, but rather in what Christ has already done on the cross 2000 years ago. He told me that I needed to trust in Christ and not in my own strength. That day I prayed and said, "God, I've sincerely tried to overcome jealousy, but I have failed miserably. Now I'm trusting in Your Son for my victory over jealousy. I can't overcome this problem in my life, but You have already overcome it. So, today I'm trusting Jesus to be my victor over jealousy.

Guess what happened? I found victory. But I've discovered that it's not a one time leap of faith. Victory is a daily walk of faith. I've had to learn that every morning when I awaken, I need to trust in Jesus. I need to say to Him as I begin each day, "God, I'm trusting You to be my victory over jealousy." When I do that, I walk in victory. But when I try to live the Christian life in my own power, I'm defeated.

Jesus makes me secure. True victory over jealousy comes when we have no other rock upon which to stand. It comes when He alone is our Fortress, when He is our all. When Christ in a very practical way is our very life, then overcoming jealousy is no longer a major problem for us. There's a sense of security that comes only from resting in Him. It calms the deep confusion of the soul. When He is our life, then nothing can shake us. We are "more than conquerors through Christ."

Jealousy and insecurity tremble in the presence of Jesus. Fear flees at the mention of His name. He is strong and mighty. He has overcome. He will give us His victory over jealousy as we trust in Him.

32

VICTORY OVER MATERIALISM

One of the most interesting developments in the world today is the extremely rapid growth of the church in the developing nations and the lack of church growth in the wealthy countries. One can only ask if there is any correlation to the prosperity of the West and the lack of substantial growth in the church. If the Western church has all the resources to reach people with the message of the gospel, then one can only wonder what has kept it from accomplishing its task.

Wealth doesn't ensure that the kingdom of God will come to a community, church, or nation. God's kingdom isn't built on the foundation of material possessions. The kingdom of God is built on righteousness. That's why Jesus said, "But seek first His kingdom and His righteousness, and all these things will be given to you as well" (Matt. 6:33). As I travel throughout developing nations, I've found a church that's seeking first God's kingdom. They don't always have nice edifices or beautiful stained glass windows. But they have peace, joy, and love in God's Spirit, which is more valuable than all the material possessions that anyone could ever acquire.

Let me be clear – being wealthy is not necessarily sinful. Money isn't the "root of all evil." It's the love of money that produces all kinds of evil. I've met some poor people who are extremely materialistic. It's not the amount of wealth that one has that makes him materialistic. It's a person's heart attitude towards material possessions that determines whether he is materialistic. Materialism is one of the most subtle temptations that any Christian will ever face.

How do we overcome such subtlety? First, we must keep our focus on Jesus. Seek Christ first. Our attitude towards wealth must be one that says, "I want God more than I desire anything else in my life. I want to know Him and walk in sweet fellowship with Christ." The real test of that attitude is whether we can be content with or without possessions. The Apostle Paul was able to know such contentment because his contentment was in Christ alone. It didn't matter whether he had much or little. He knew contentment that came from the intimate knowledge of God.

Not only must Christ be first in our lives, but our hearts must seek after His kingdom. One of the reasons that God required the tithe of the children of Israel was to remind them who it was that had provided for them. God gave them everything they possessed. He met every need of theirs. But they were to always keep His kingdom first. They were to first take care of those things that pertained to His kingdom. As long as they did that, God would bless and provide for them.

Often the test of whether we've gotten caught up in the trap of materialism is how we view giving to the kingdom of God. If we simply tip our hats to God and flip him the leftovers of our wealth, then we've probably been snared by a spirit of materialism. But if we have kept our priorities straight, putting Him before our own wants and desires, He will meet every need we have and keep us from any spirit of materialism.

A final safeguard against a materialistic spirit is seeking God's righteousness. What would it take for you to compromise God's commandments? How much money would it take for you to tell a "little white lie?" What Biblical principle would you violate in order to have more things? We will overcome materialism only when we have a rock solid commitment to Christ's righteousness. We must seek Christ first and His kingdom, and we must maintain an unwavering commitment to living in a righteous and Christlike manner. Only then will we know victory over materialism.

33

VICTORY OVER AN UNBRIDLED TONGUE

One year prior to the collapse of the Soviet Union, I preached the first national crusade in Moldova, one of the former republics of the USSR. There was a great sense of expectation. No one knew what to expect when I preached in the national stadium that first Sunday. The atmosphere was charged. The news media was present to capture that historic moment.

One reporter had an extremely relevant question. "Do you really think that you can change lives simply through your words?" she quizzically asked. I pondered the question. I realized that she had grown up as an atheist. She lived in a nation where everyone was taught that there is no God. It must have seemed incredible to her that I would attempt to change lives and even a nation through the mere use of public speaking. Soviet citizens were used to lives being changed by the power of military weapons – not the power of words.

I responded to the reporter, "Yes, I believe that we will see lives changed by the words that I speak today." I could speak so confidently, not because of the eloquence of my speech, but because of the power of the message of the gospel that I would deliver that day. There have been enough years to pass since that day that I am able to reflect on my response and know if it was an accurate one.

The editor of the first Christian magazine in Moldova

is a woman whose life was changed by the message I delivered that day. There are several missionaries and Christian workers who were atheists before they heard that message. Men and women have travelled to other regions of the former Soviet Union because of what they heard that day. Yes, mere words were able to change the entire direction of hundreds and even thousands of lives in that one day.

When one thinks of the power of words, it should cause us to be extremely careful about which words we use. Words can be used to build up or to tear down. Words can bring life and peace or death and destruction. The person who learns to bless others with their words will be a very wise person and find that they have contributed greatly to their families and to society.

The Scriptures say, "If anyone considers himself religious and yet does not keep a tight rein on his tongue, he deceives himself and his religion is worthless" (James 1:26). The test of the purity of our hearts lies in the use of our words. How we use our tongues actually tells what kind of Christianity we are living. If we can have victory in this area of our lives, then we can probably conquer any spiritual foe we face.

We can build or destroy a child's esteem by the words we speak. We can construct a healthy marriage or destroy deep relationships through our communication. It's imperative to bring this little instrument, the human tongue, under the control of the Holy Spirit. But the question is, "How do we do that?"

First, speak the truth. Jesus is the truth. When we speak of the Saviour, we will be able to see lives changed for eternity. When the Holy Spirit works in our lives, He will always glorify Jesus. Therefore, we ought to speak of the Saviour every opportunity that we get. Second, speak that which blesses people, rather than curses them. Say those things which will build people up rather than tear them down. Third, when you begin to feel anger, then place a bridle over your tongue. Determine that when you are angry that you will count to thirty before you respond. Often much damage is done because we speak too quickly. Finally, ask the Holy Spirit to take control of your speech. Ask Him to give you the power to speak only those things which please the Father.

As we give control of our tongues to God, we will not only find pure faith, but we will also see lives changed. Yes, lives can be changed by the words we speak – if we speak in the power of the Holy Spirit and only that which honours and pleases God.

34

VICTORY OVER DECEIT

Recently, the President of the United States confessed that he had "an inappropriate relationship" with Monica Lewinsky, an intern at the White House, and that he had "misled people." Citizens of the United States immediately began to debate whether President Clinton should remain in the highest position of the country. Some said that he should be removed from office while others said that he should resign. However, one thing became clear to everyone – the American baby boomer generation has become used to deceit being a normal part of life.

What is deceit, and why is it so wrong? How does one find victory over deceit if it has been a part of their character? First, we need to understand that truth and deceit are incompatible. They can't live in the same house. In fact, deceit is often the withholding of truth. It's telling partial truth but not "the truth, the whole truth, and nothing but the truth." Deceit is somewhat different from lying, in that a lie is a direct contradiction of the truth. Deceit is much more subtle. It simply doesn't give a full disclosure of the truth and is usually rooted in selfish ambition.

Justice is built upon truth, and without it, there can be no justice. Once truth is compromised, then justice ceases to exist. That's why the actions of President Clinton were so grave. If truth doesn't have its way, then the entire American system of justice collapses. If that were to happen, then it would only be a matter of time for the United States to cease to be a nation that leads in world affairs.

But there's an even more critical issue for the Christian. The goal in the life of the believer is to become like Christ. One particular description of Jesus in the Bible continually amazes me. John, inspired by the Holy Spirit, described Jesus, saying that He was "full of grace and truth" (John 1:14). In the debate over the President of the United States, we hear two distinct voices being raised. One demands truth. The other cries for grace. One says that justice is the issue. The other claims forgiveness is that which is needed.

But when we look to the Saviour, we see absolute truth and perfect grace. He carries justice in one hand and forgiveness in the other. There is no partial truth nor any incomplete forgiveness in Him. The standard for the Christian is not the American judicial system (or any other political system). It's not the opinion polls of the day. The standard is absolute purity and perfection. It's full forgiveness. It's simply Jesus. There's no deceit in Him. He is absolute and total truth. If we are to know His forgiveness, then we must come clean about the dirt in our lives. There's no room for half truths. They only lead to total deception.

If we are to experience victory over deceit, then we must learn to be painfully honest. John wrote in his first epistle, "If we claim to be without sin, we deceive ourselves and the truth is not in us. If we confess our sins, He is faithful and just and will forgive us our sins and purify us from all unrighteousness" (1 John 1:8,9). Notice how interconnected truth, justice, and forgiveness are in that passage, and observe how related denial and deceit are. The victorious Christian life is one lived in the light of the truth. Victory can only be seen in the spotlight of truth.

35

VICTORY OVER BAD HABITS

Everyone develops habits in their lives, good ones and bad ones. However, the phrase, "that's just a bad habit," can often be a cover up for a long term pattern of sin. In fact, the "bad habit" is often a stronghold in our lives to which Satan has access. Consequently, he is able to keep us from the victory that Jesus wrought 2000 years ago. A bad habit is a physical pattern which can be harmful to us and displeasing to God. Often, it's something that has been haunting us since childhood. How do these habits get into our lives, and how can we know freedom from them?

First, we need to understand that not all habits are bad. We often have good habits that are necessary to function in the manner in which we were created. If we eat regularly and consistently, then that's a good habit and a part of our natural makeup. However, if we eat obsessively, then eating becomes a bad habit and is ultimately destructive. A bad habit can be an extreme action of something which is normally healthy.

Some people think that if we have enough will power, then we can overcome our bad habits. It's true that some people seem to have an enormous amount of will power. However, I've never met anyone who has the ability to overcome all their bad behaviour patterns. The only human with that kind of ability to ever grace this planet is Jesus. He alone holds the key to victory over every bad habit in life. Only Jesus can set us free from bad habits that stalk us.

When I was a single university student, I met a beautiful girl who was attempting to be elected Freshman Class Secretary. She was originally from the state of Texas. Therefore, she acquired the nickname "Tex." She had as beautiful an inward personality as she did outward looks. But she had one very serious bad habit – she smoked constantly. Smoking had been a part of her actions since high school and she knew that it would ultimately destroy her body.

One night, after God had been speaking to her heart, she went to her dorm room and cried out to God, "Oh, God, I need you. I place my faith in your Son, Jesus. Come and dwell in my heart." In that moment, a miracle took place. No, she didn't see a flash of lightning or hand writing on a wall. But the King of kings took residence in her life. He became the source of her victory over smoking. What she was unable to do by human will power, He did in her by God's power. She began to experience victory. Even though Satan had a stronghold on her through tobacco, he was no match for God.

I've seen alcoholics find freedom from their addiction through Christ. I have watched the most hardened drug abusers discover victory over drug addiction by the power of Jesus. It doesn't matter what a person's habit may be, Jesus provides the victory over every bad habit – no matter how large or small it may be. It doesn't matter how impossible it may seem to overcome the habit, it's not too big for God. He specializes in the impossible. Jesus said, "With men this is impossible; but with God all things are possible" (Matt. 19:26 KJV). What habit continues to drag you down to defeat? Look to Jesus. He will raise you to victory over any bad habit.

36

BRING EVERY THOUGHT CAPTIVE

Most of the struggles that we face in life are inner ones. The outward battles are normally a result of deep inner conflicts that have been built over a lifetime. If we are to truly experience victory over bad habits and wrong patterns of actions, then we must learn to undergo a transformation of our inner thoughts and feelings. The Apostle Paul wrote to the church in Corinth saying, "We demolish arguments and every pretension that sets itself up against the knowledge of God, and we take captive every thought to make it obedient to Christ" (2 Cor. 10:5 NIV).

Paul was speaking of the spiritual battle that every Christian faces. He understood that the greatest conflicts of life are spiritual ones, and that the battleground is often the mind of the believer. Before a person comes to know Christ in a deeply personal way, the Bible says that he is a captive or slave to sin. In other words, our entire outlook and view of life is built upon attitudes and thought patterns that are contrary to God's plan for us. We build those patterns of thoughts over months and even years. When we come to know Christ, that doesn't mean that we no longer have to deal with wrong thought patterns. It simply means that we are no longer slaves to those patterns.

But we must learn to "take every thought to make it obedient to Christ." Let me explain. I grew up in a home where I experienced a lot of negativism. My mother was very critical. There's a fine line of difference between a critical spirit and an analytical spirit. A critical spirit analyses each situation and condemns. But an analytical spirit is able to discern right from wrong and find an appropriate means of action to do the right thing. Over many years, I turned a God-given analytical spirit into a self-centred critical spirit. My first line of thought about anyone or any type of action was always a negative, critical one.

When Christ came into my life, He set me free from such a critical spirit. I was no longer a captive to such thinking, no longer a slave. However, I had not built a negative spirit within my heart in one moment. I had built such a pattern of thinking over a lifetime. Therefore, I needed to learn to tear down that stronghold in my life brick by brick. That simply meant that every day I needed to take every negative thought captive unto the obedience of Christ.

When I awaken every morning, my "natural" way of thinking is a negative one. I, therefore, take time in my time alone with God to ask Him to capture every thought of mine. Through prayer, I bring every thought captive unto the obedience of Christ. I ask God to fill me with those thoughts which are pleasing to Him. The more regularly that I bring my thought patterns under Christ's rule, the quicker that stronghold is torn down in my life.

Once that stronghold is torn down, it doesn't mean that I am no longer tempted in that area. It simply means that Satan no longer has a foothold in that area of my life. I don't have to be a "naturally negative" person. I can be a supernaturally positive person. No matter what comes my way, I have been given everything I need to overwhelmingly conquer those patterns of thought that are so contrary to the character and ways of God. Each of us can experience victory over wrong thought patterns. God has given you weapons of spiritual warfare to overcome Satan's stronghold on your life. Begin today to bring every thought captive unto the obedience of Christ.

37

VICTORY OVER THE FEAR OF REJECTION

A number of years ago, I was visiting a family of mountain climbers in what was then East Germany. They wanted me to see a very beautiful part of their country. The only problem was that we had to climb a very high mountain, and I had a fear of heights. However, they assured me that it was very safe and that we could climb the mountain on a secure trail. Therefore, two American friends and I agreed to go with them.

Everything was just as they had told me, until we got about 50 meters from the top of the mountain. We, then, had to start pulling ourselves over rocks and begin genuine mountain climbing. Something snapped in me. All of a sudden, I grabbed a rock and held on for my life. No one saw me because I was the last one. When everyone reached the top, I could hear everyone saying, "Oh, look how beautiful!" Then I heard someone say, "Where's Sammy?"

They looked down and saw me frantically holding on to the rock. I couldn't move. I was paralysed. They said, "Come on up, Sammy. It's fantastic up here." All I could say was, "I can't move!" After much debate, my friends had to finally pull my fingers off the rock and carry me down the mountain. It was one of the most embarrassing moments of my life.

But I learned a great lesson that day. I learned the power

of the human emotion of fear. Fear had literally crippled me. Since that day, I've watched fear paralyse many people. I've seen people rendered immobile because of the fear of failure, the fear of the future, and the fear of death. Perhaps the greatest and most common crippling fear that I've seen is that of the fear of rejection. I've seen people do harm to their own bodies because of this fear. I've watched people compromise their morals, trample their beliefs, and become spiritually defeated because of this fear.

There's one great solution to fear – love (perfect love). The Bible says, "There is no fear in love. But perfect love drives out fear, because fear has to do with punishment. The one who fears is not made perfect in love" (I John 4:18 NIV). There is only one place in all of human history where "perfect love" can be found – the cross. Outside Jerusalem, on a hill, between two thieves, suspended between heaven and earth hung the perfect Son of God. He cried out those words that would ring throughout history as the perfect love of God, "Father, forgive them...."

Only Jesus had the ability to forgive those who hated Him, those who were the very enemies of God. He loved all of mankind with the perfect love of God. He loved you and me with perfect love. It's that love that casts out the fear of rejection. It's that love that allows us to know, feel, and experience God's acceptance. Jesus said, "All that the Father gives Me shall come to Me, and the one who comes to Me I will certainly not cast out" (John 6:37 NASB). When we come to Jesus, we encounter the perfect love of God and fear has to flee.

If you find yourself a captive to the fear of rejection, then come to the cross. You'll find there the perfect love of God that will release you to be all that God intended you to be. Courage flows from the cross. The cross permeates the innermost parts of your life and enables you to see God in His infinite love. Look to the cross! Live near the cross! Take up your cross! Follow Jesus!

38

VICTORY OVER LEGALISM

After speaking several years ago to a group of Christian leaders, a man said to me, "I really disagree with you. I don't think that God's law is good. That's what brings condemnation to our lives."

I quickly came to realize that this gentleman had an improper understanding of God's law. Everything that God gives to man is good because God is good. That's a part of His nature. He gave His law for our good. He created us. Therefore, He knows how we ought to live. He knows our structure, our frame. When He gave His law, it was to instruct us in a happy, healthy life. For instance, when He told the Jews not to eat pork, it wasn't because He was looking for a reason to hit them over the head if they disobeyed Him. He gave those instructions because He had created everything that exists. He knew what would produce disease and death and what would cause life and health. The law of God is good and enriches our lives.

However, the Scripture teaches us that we are to live under the rule of the Holy Spirit rather than under the letter of the law. Many religious leaders didn't understand this during the times of Christ. The same is true today. Religious leaders wanted to stone Him because He healed people on the Sabbath. Jesus told them that the Sabbath was made for man, and not man for the Sabbath. He understood the purpose and intent of the law. The religious leaders only knew the letter of the law. Those who follow only the letter of the law and ignore the spirit of the law fall into the trap of legalism. Legalism ultimately produces defeat.

A few years ago, the President of the United States admitted to having an improper sexual relationship, but at the same time he instructed his lawyers to split legal hairs about the definition of a "sexual relationship." Such legalism brought condemnation from members of his own party and ultimately left a bad taste in the mouth of the general population. He was arguing the letter of the law, but ignoring the spirit of the law.

Many Christians have done the same thing. Legalism always leads to defeat. That's why the Bible instructs us to live by the power of the Holy Spirit. When we live by the Spirit, we are not under the rule of the law. That doesn't mean that we ignore the law or violate the law. It simply means that we fulfil the deep purposes of the law. In other words we do the will of God from the depths of our hearts.

A person who lives under the rule of the Holy Spirit is truly a free person. This person is not only faithful to his spouse, but he's free from the lusts that drag him into immorality. That's true victory – one that's in the heart and works its way into our everyday lives. But when someone attempts to live by the letter of the law, he's on a one way street to defeat.

A victorious Christian is one who has learned to yield his life to the rule of the Holy Spirit. He is not in bondage to legalistic definitions. He's free to be all that God intended him to be. He fulfils much more than the letter of the law. A victorious Christian fulfils the spirit and intent of the law because his obedience is an outflow of the indwelling presence of the Holy Spirit. When we live by the power of the Holy Spirit, the law no longer is an issue in our lives because we will accomplish God's ultimate purpose in our lives. Victory over legalism flows from following the leadership of the Holy Spirit.

39

THE PURSUIT OF HOLINESS

Holiness seems to be a word that has been lost in the modern Christian vocabulary, and it's rarely understood by the 21st century believer. Yet, the Scripture states emphatically, "Follow peace with all men, and holiness, without which no man shall see the Lord" (Heb 12:14 KJV). It's impossible to see God without holiness of heart and life. We'll never see and know the victory that He gives to us without holiness. We'll not know the glory of God without holiness. If we desire to see God at work in our lives, then we must diligently pursue holiness.

What is holiness and how do we get it? Biblical holiness stems from a Greek word which basically means "a life that is set apart for God." A person can't be holy in life and conduct while attempting to hold on to God with one hand and the world with the other one. A holy life is one that has surrendered completely to God. That doesn't mean that a person is perfect. It simple means that he has given his life to God and is in the process of being perfected.

Holiness of life actually begins with holiness pursuing us and is continued by our pursuing it. Holiness is a process that begins at the moment of conversion. When Christ's Spirit enters our hearts, then holiness enters our lives because His Spirit is the Holy Spirit. It's at that moment that a process is begun – conformity unto the image of Christ. It's a lifelong process.

It's important that we understand two basic principles. First, we can't make ourselves holy. That's the deep work of the Holy Spirit in our lives. On the other hand we must pursue holiness of life. We must seek after the Holy Spirit's work to make us conformed unto the image of Christ. The Greek word used in Hebrews 12:14 that says we should "follow peace with all men and holiness" is one that is often used of a hunter seeking and pursuing his prey. We, too, are exhorted to pursue holiness in the same manner – that is with diligence.

We have all the resources that we need to become holy. We have the indwelling Holy Spirit, the Bible, Christ's victory on the cross, and Christian fellowship. Why then do we need to pursue holiness? These wonderful resources must never be taken for granted. If our lives are going to be victorious, then we must fervently seek holiness. For instance, because of Christ's death on the cross, we have fellowship with one another. Yet, we still need to seek a church (a fellowship of believers) where we can interact and grow in our faith. The same is true with holiness of life. Because of the indwelling presence of the Holy Spirit, we have everything we need for victory in life. Yet we still need to pursue God's Spirit leading and empowering us to live that victory.

The believer is called to be a follower. As we pursue the Holy Spirit's leading in our lives, we will be conformed supernaturally into the image of Christ. That's the strategy of the Christian for victory. We simply set out in pursuit of the Holy Spirit. We obey His leading. We follow His guidance. The end result is holiness of life and purity of heart. Our conduct becomes that which is pleasing unto God. The Christian life begins with holiness pursuing us, but victory is maintained as we pursue holiness.

40

PRIDE – HINDRANCE TO HOLINESS

Holiness of life should be the goal of every Christian. Holiness is simply conformity unto the image of Christ. It's one of the great attributes of victorious Christians throughout the centuries. Bishop J. C. Ryle wrote in his book *Christian Leaders of the 18th Century* that leaders during the great revivals of the past were always holy men and women. They had their faults and blind spots like anyone else, but they had a heart desire to be like Christ. They wanted to know Him intimately.

Anyone who wishes to be like Christ will have a heart of humility. Humility and holiness walk down the same path. However, there's no room for pride in the heart that's in hot pursuit of holiness. Holiness looks Godward while pride gazes selfward. The perfect picture of holiness is Christ. The best portrait of pride is Lucifer. Holiness is the desire to be like Christ. Pride is the aspiration to be better than others. Holiness manifests meekness of character. Pride brags of brashness and has no character.

It's impossible to walk in holiness and maintain a heart of pride. Arrogance and pride are simply hindrances to a holy heart. When we understand what a holy heart is, then it's easy to see how impossible it is for pride and holiness to dwell in the same heart. Holiness is simply the inward work of God in the believer to be conformed to Christ. He existed in eternity as God. Yet, the very nature of Jesus was humility. He humbled Himself to the point of taking upon Himself the clothes of humanity. Jesus, the Son of

God and Son of man, can only be described in terms of absolute humility. Therefore, it's impossible to be proud and at the same time to be like Christ.

The Bible says that "God is opposed to the proud, but gives grace to the humble." If God is opposed to the proud, then it is impossible to be holy and to be proud. Many times we dress our pride up in different styles. We mistakenly believe that some kind of pride is okay. However, the book of Proverbs says that God hates pride. It doesn't matter whether it's religious pride, spiritual pride, ethnic pride, or racial pride. Every form of pride has its roots in comparison to other people. But holiness only looks to Jesus. Therefore, we can't be proud and be holy. Pride actually becomes a hindrance to the process of holiness.

Pride often is at the root of other sins. On several occasions, when I have found myself confessing my sins and asking God to search my heart, I discovered that at the root of some sin that was plaguing my life was pride. God allowed me to fall in order to show me what was in my heart. Pride is at the heart of evil in this world. Lucifer was cast out of heaven because he became proud. Adam and Eve were cast out of the garden because of pride. You and I are knocked off the highway of holiness when we allow ourselves to become proud.

Let me encourage you to take a few minutes and pray the prayer of the Psalmist: "Search my heart, Oh God, and see if there be any wickedness in me." Ask God to expose any seed of pride that might be lying dormant. Ask Him to free you from the self life. A broken heart and contrite spirit will not be despised by God. He longs to see a humble heart. He places that heart on the highway of holiness.

41

HUMILITY – THE SECRET TO HOLINESS

Occasionally, I hear someone say, "He's one of those holier than thou guys." When people make such a statement they don't realize the absolute contradiction of what they have said. A holy heart will always be a humble heart. Holiness doesn't compare itself to others. Holiness only looks to Jesus. Therefore, it's impossible to "be holier than thou." Holiness of life grows in the soil of a humble heart.

There are several reasons why humility of heart is the secret to holiness of life and conduct. First, humility is the essence of the life of Christ. Jesus existed in eternity as God. Yet, He humbled Himself by becoming a man. He clothed Himself with human flesh. He stooped so low that He would become like us in order that we could know Him. There's never been in human history such an example of humility. God became a man. That's who Jesus is – the God-man. Even the name given to Him, Emmanuel, means God with us.

If the goal of holiness is to become like Christ, then we must clothe ourselves with humility. Christ is the epitome of humility. Therefore, we must seek to be humble in heart and life. Christ lived an absolutely holy life, and He was the perfect picture of humility. Therefore, if we are to become holy, we too must humble ourselves under God's mighty hand.

But there's another reason why humility is a necessity to holiness. It's impossible for us in our own power to achieve holiness of life. Holiness of life can only be made a reality by the grace of God. We become what God wants us to become by God's grace. And grace is only applied to the humble heart. The Bible says, "God is opposed to the proud, but gives grace to the humble."

A pastor friend of mine once spent forty days praying and fasting. After his time with God, I asked him what God had shown him during that intense time of seeking God. His response was quite interesting. "God showed me that I could never again say, 'I'd never do that,' " he said. "When I would see someone commit adultery I used to say, 'I'd never do that.' But God showed me that in my flesh dwells no good thing. I can only say, 'By God's grace, I will never do that.' "

What God showed my friend was quite simple but deeply profound. The only reason why any Christian can claim victory over sins in their lives is because of the grace of God. We are what we are by the grace of God. We become more like Christ because of the grace of God. It's not our will power or our ability to overcome evil. It's by God's grace that we know and experience victory of life and holiness of conduct.

When the seed of humility is planted in our hearts, it will be watered by the grace of God. The Holy Spirit will make sure that it grows. When humility comes to full maturity, it blossoms into a beautiful bouquet of holiness. Our life and conduct will reflect the beauty of Christ's character. Humility is the secret to holiness.

42

GRACE AND GROWTH

Have you ever seen two people make a commitment to Christ, and one of them really grows in his faith while the other one struggles in his walk with God? Have you ever wondered what made the difference in the two people? There's a simple one-word answer to those questions – grace. When I first came to know Christ, I began to grow rapidly in my faith. There was a fire burning deep within my soul. Many of my friends, however, endeavoured to grow but were without success.

One of my friends came to me and said, "Sammy, you must have a lot of will power. That must be why you are growing so much in your walk with God." I knew what my friend was saying wasn't true, but at that time I didn't know why. I just knew that I didn't have enough will power to change many of the things that had changed in my life. The more I learned about God, the more I concluded that there was only one reason for my growth – God's grace.

But why didn't my friends grow in the same way? Many of them were from Christian backgrounds. They knew the Bible. They didn't have the same heart to learn that I had. They had grown up in Sunday School and many felt that they knew everything there was to know about the Christian life. On the other hand, I knew that I didn't know anything. I was quite aware that I needed to depend completely upon God. And God gives grace to the humble (1 Pet. 5:5, Jas. 4:6). It's that grace that produces spiritual growth.

Without grace, we can never become what God intends

us to become. We are saved by God's grace, and we continue to grow by His grace. We can see a direct correlation with the condition of our hearts and our growth. A humble heart is able to receive grace. When grace is applied to our hearts, then the more we become like Christ. In reality, the older we get, the more like Jesus we should become.

The world in which we live judges people by their outward appearance. However, the Bible says that God looks upon the inner man. When grace is applied to our hearts, then we become more beautiful in God's sight. That's why many of my heroes have been those who have walked with God for many years. There's an inner beauty that can only be described in spiritual terms. There's a quality of peace and love that seems to exude from their lives that has been produced by years of God's grace being applied to their hearts. They are the giants of the faith.

Yet, I have also seen elderly people (including Christians) who are bitter and very unhappy people. Their very personalities have been scarred by years of attempting to live in the power of the "flesh." The difference over many years, between a person who has allowed God's grace to be applied to his heart and one that has not, is like night and day. There's an old saying about "growing old gracefully." There's only one way to "grow old gracefully" – be full of grace as you grow old.

Yes, it's truly amazing grace that saves us, but it's also amazing grace that keeps us. And, perhaps just as amazing is the grace that causes us to grow into the image of Christ. If you want to become more beautiful every day, then humble yourself under God's mighty hand, and His grace will be applied to you. You'll become more beautiful every year – even with wrinkles on your face!

43

VICTORY BRINGS GREATER GROWTH

There's an interesting principle of life – victory produces more victory and defeat produces greater defeat. It doesn't always have to be this way. But, unless the cycle is broken, it's merely a fact of life. Success births greater success and failure births more failure. However, in the Christian life the cycle of failure and defeat can be halted by the Holy Spirit dwelling in the believer. He can give us victory over any patterns that we have developed.

There's a reason in the Christian life that victory produces greater victories. Jesus said, "He that hath my commandments, and keepeth them, he it is that loveth me: and he that loveth me shall be loved of my Father, and I will love him, and will manifest myself to him" (John 14:21 KJV). When we walk in obedience to God, Jesus promises to manifest Himself to us. It is the manifest presence of Jesus that enables us to overcome sin in our lives. Jesus is our victory. Therefore, the more we obey Him – the more we experience His manifest presence. The more we experience His presence – the more we are empowered to do His will. What a wonderful cycle in which we can live life!

Every step of obedience to God produces fruit within our lives. That's why the Scriptures say that we live from faith to faith and glory to glory. One step of obedience leads to another step of obedience. After walking up a number of those steps, we find ourselves on a higher level of our relationship with Christ. We go from one level of faith to another. We experience one level of God's glory and are enabled to go on to another level. That makes the Christian life an ongoing adventure with Christ.

When I first became a Christian, I was thrilled with the fullness of walking with Christ. I remember thinking to myself, "It just can't get any better than this." Yet it has gotten better. I told my wife before we were married, "I can't promise you that we will ever be rich, but I promise you this – life won't be boring." And it definitely hasn't been boring! I'm writing this devotional on a plane flying towards the Amazon region in Brazil to preach the glorious gospel of Jesus Christ! I had no clue what God would do with my life over the past 36 years of walking with Jesus. And it just keeps getting better and better. Victory begets victory!

But you may be asking, "What if a person is in the opposite cycle – what does he do? Defeat produces a cycle of more defeat. Is that person doomed to failure?" This is the great thing about the Christian life. No matter how defeated a person has been in his life, Christ can change that at any moment. The grace of God is greater than the worst of sin. The cycle can be changed. The believer in Christ has every resource needed to overcome the most terrible cycles in our lives. The Holy Spirit dwells deep within our hearts to empower us to become like Christ.

We must confess our sins and truly repent of them. The blood of Jesus is sufficient to cleanse us from all unrighteousness – no matter how bad our sins may seem. Once we have confessed and are clean, we can appropriate by faith the Holy Spirit to empower us to walk in obedience to the Word of God. We take each act of obedience one step at a time. Before long, we find ourselves on a new cycle – one of victory. Victory leads to victory. That's why Paul wrote that "we are more than conquerors through Christ who loved us".

Begin the cycle of victory today. Take it one step at a time. You'll find yourself going from victory to victory; faith to faith; and glory to glory!

44

THE PURPOSE OF LIFE

The ultimate test of the victorious Christian life is whether a person has done with his life what he was created to do. The proof of victory comes when we cross the finish line of life and step into eternity. It's when we hear those words from heaven, "Well done, thou good and faithful servant." Victorious Christian living is always in accord with our purpose in life.

Unfortunately, many people have no idea what their purpose in life should be. When the former Soviet Union collapsed, my wife and I were travelling to Siberia and had to stay overnight in Moscow. We stayed in the home of a lady who was an atheist. She was a professor in the university. She asked us what we would be doing in Siberia. When I told her that we were going to speak to people about Christ, she asked what subject I would speak on. When I told her that I was going to speak the first day on the purpose of life, she became very animated and exclaimed, "Oh, I wish I could go to hear you. I don't have any purpose in life."

That lady is like most people that I have met. They have no idea why they were created. They were born, grow up, get a job, get married, have children, grow old, and die. Yet, many have never even considered why they were created. They are some of the most disillusioned people in life. They are like a man in the centre of New York City who is lost. He walks up to a policeman and asks him for help. The policeman then asks the man where he wants to go. The man replies, "I don't know." Many people are just like that in life. They don't have any idea where they are headed in life.

But others have a purpose. It's just the wrong purpose. They're frantically trying to climb the ladder of success, popularity, or power. They think that their accumulation of wealth, fame, or position is the true purpose of life. However, they will be the most disappointed in life. They won't be able to take their money, houses, cars, or friends with them into eternity. They are like a person who has a ladder, and he puts it against a wall and climbs it as fast as he can. However, when he gets to the top of the wall, he discovers that he put his ladder against the wrong wall.

But there's a third kind of person when it comes to the purpose of life. It's the person who has found the true purpose of life. This person is the most fulfilled. But that brings up an extremely important question. What is the real purpose of life? When life is over, what should we have accomplished? Jesus gave the simple but profound answer to that question when He said, "Love the Lord your God with all your heart and with all your soul and with all your mind. This is the first and greatest commandment. And the second is like it: 'Love your neighbour as yourself'" (Matt. 22:37-39 NIV).

The real purpose of life is as simple as that – love God with all your heart and love your neighbour as yourself. The world would be a much better place in which to live if all did those two things. Ultimately, the victorious Christian life will be judged by how we loved God and loved others. It's out of that sense of purpose that the rest of our victory flows.

45

PRIORITIES IN LIFE

Many people begin the Christian life experiencing victory only to find themselves defeated after a few years of walking with God. I've watched men and women surrender to God's call on their lives. They live with excitement and enthusiasm for Christ and do what He has called them to do. Yet, years later they can be found on the sidelines of the battle for the kingdom of God. What happens to these many well-meaning believers? Some of us may even ask, "What's happened to me?"

Often, we get tripped up in the life and work to which God has called us because of misplaced priorities. We begin well, but finish poorly because we didn't keep "the main thing – the main thing." We get sidetracked chasing interesting looking rabbits that lead us nowhere. Often we settle for rabbit stew when God has prepared a banquet of sirloin steak for us.

In order to maintain correct priorities, we have to always keep our focus on God's purpose in our lives. There are seasons in everyone's life. It's often in the change of the seasons of life that our priorities change. For instance, my wife and I went through a seasonal change a few years ago. Our youngest child, Renee, left home to go away to study at the university. Thus, my wife was able to begin travelling with me. Therefore, I stepped up the pace of my travel and speaking schedule. As long as our children were home and unable to travel with me, I placed a self-imposed limit on my travel. However, since the season has changed, I now have the liberty to travel more often.

I know God's purpose for my life is first to love Him with all my heart, mind, and soul. Second, it's to love my neighbour as myself. My closest and most important neighbour is my family. Therefore, they take high priority in my life – higher than my ministry. I've seen many people lose everything – their ministry and family because of misplaced priorities. You may be wondering what a Christian's priorities should be. I'm convinced that the victorious Christian will have priorities which will look something like this:

The number one priority is – my walk with God.

Second – my walk with my family.

Third – my work and ministry.

I've seen many people establish incorrect priorities and eventually find themselves defeated. Our seasons of life may change, but our purpose in life must remain constant. And our priorities in life must always be built around the eternal purpose that God has for each of us. Priorities tell the truth about what's really important to us. We can say that we love God with all of our hearts. But the true test of that love will be revealed in the priorities which we have established and continue to refine as the seasons of life change.

Priorities find their expression in time spent. Our time should be spent doing what is important to us. Some people want to do that, but they don't muster the courage to do that which is important. Establishing priorities in our lives and living by them is a courageous act. But such courage will produce victory in our daily lives. Take that step today and begin to establish God-given priorities in your life. It pays benefits for years to come.

46

THE PURSUIT OF GOD

When I walked into church that Sunday evening, I wasn't seeking after God, but His Spirit was certainly pursuing me. My only motivation for going to church that night was to be with my girlfriend. Her father said that if I didn't go to church, then I couldn't see his daughter. That was an easy choice. I went to church. I was taken by surprise that evening when something began to stir in my heart. I became convinced of my guilt and shame before a holy God, and I was strangely drawn to seek forgiveness through Jesus.

After coming to Christ and experiencing His grace being applied to my heart, I was consumed with a desire to know Him more. I began to seek after Christ. The very fact that I wanted to know Him was a result of His initial pursuit of me. Herein lies a great truth for the Christian – our pursuit of God is simply the fruit of His pursuit of us. We must never forget that the only reason that we even desire to know Him is because He first loved us and gave Himself for us. We seek Him because He sought us.

Our victory is an extension of His victory achieved in our hearts. In order to walk in and maintain that victory, we must earnestly pursue God. Jesus said, "Ask and it will be given to you; seek and you will find; knock and the door will be opened to you" (Matt. 7:7 NIV). The verb tense in the Greek language connotes a continuous asking and seeking. In other words, we are to pursue God. There ought to be an intense desire to know God intimately.

There are two ways in which we need to pursue God. First, we need to pursue Him in prayer. It's in the intimate quiet moments alone with Him that we ought to "ask, seek, and knock." The passage in Matthew chapter 7 is a prayer passage. We are asking, seeking, and knocking when we come into His presence in prayer. Many Christians only ask for handouts when they pray. They are not interested in seeking God's face. They are more interested in seeking His hand. The hand of God is wonderful. But nothing can compare with the face of God.

When we seek the hand of God, we are wanting Him to do something for us. When we seek the face of God, we are desiring to get to know Him. It's this desiring to know Him intimately that is the pursuit of God. Our heart's desire and number one priority in prayer ought to be to have fellowship with God. Sadly, few Christians approach prayer in this manner. Most Christians are interested in the hand of God rather than seeking the face of God.

The second way in which we need to pursue God is in His holiness. Jesus said, "He that has my commandments, and keeps them, he it is that loves me: and he that loves me shall be loved of my Father, and I will love him, and will manifest myself to him" (John 14:21 KJV). We come to know God as we obey His word. Jesus said that we love Him when we obey Him. As we love Him, He manifests or makes Himself known unto us. We get to know God in His uniqueness, His character, and His attributes as we walk in obedience to His commands.

Spend some time alone with God in prayer. Have only one purpose for that time – getting to know God. Read His word. Purpose in your heart that you will obey all that He has shown you. That's the pursuit of God. There's no greater pursuit known to mankind – not the pursuit of happiness, wealth, or fame. It's seeking after God that produces fulfilment in life. Pursue God. In Him is abundance of joy.

47

THE KNOWLEDGE OF GOD

One of the most remarkable statements in the Bible was made by the Apostle Paul when he said, "that I may know Him, and the power of His resurrection and the fellowship of His sufferings, being conformed to His death." Paul had already come to know Christ. While on the road to Damascus, Jesus revealed Himself to Paul. His conversion was extraordinary. No one could deny that Paul had come to know Jesus. Why, then, did Paul say that he wanted to know Jesus?

Paul's desire to know Jesus could be compared in a certain sense to my relationship with my wife. For instance, when I met her, I fell "in love" with her and we were later married. After we were married, I could say in every sense of the word that I "knew" my wife. Yet, today – over 30 years later, I can say, "I know her so much more now." I knew her 33 years ago, but I REALLY know her now. And I want to know her more. The more that I get to know her, the more that I love her. That's precisely what Paul was saying about his relationship with Jesus. He knew Jesus. He loved Jesus. But he wanted to know Him and love Him more.

There were three ways in which Paul wanted to know Jesus, and we should also desire to know Him in those ways. First, he wanted to know Jesus in the power of His resurrection. The very Power that raised Jesus from the dead is available to every believer. No one needs to be defeated. The Bible says that we have been raised with Christ and seated in heavenly places. We are victorious because of the resurrection of Christ. He has defeated every enemy known to mankind – sin, death, hell, and the devil. Therefore, we can be "more than conquerors." Paul wanted to practically know Christ in such power. Our hearts ought, also, to long to know Him in the power of His resurrection.

But Paul also wanted to know Christ in the fellowship of His sufferings. Many Christians want to know the power of God, but few want to know the sufferings of Christ. Yet, I've found the depth of the love of God can only be experienced in the midst of suffering. Often it's pain that drives us into the arms of the Saviour. Knowing Christ in the fellowship of His sufferings isn't something to be feared, rather it's a relationship with God that is to be embraced. As one author aptly put it, "Don't waste your sorrows." Don't just endure suffering, but embrace it and allow God to draw you into a deeper knowledge of Himself.

The final way in which Paul wanted to know Christ was by being made conformable to His death. The totality of the Christian life is in "putting off the old life and putting on the new man." In order to do that, we must die to self. Paul knew that the knowledge of God and a spirit of pride could not dwell in the same heart. As we get to know God better, the more we die to self. That's why John the Baptist said, "He must increase, but I must decrease" (John 3:30). To know Him is to die to our selfish wants, desires, and motivations.

The victorious Christian life is one given to getting to know Christ. To know Him is to love Him!

48

THE LOVE OF GOD

If I had to choose one attribute of God that produces victory in the lives of believers, then I would pick the attribute of love. The Bible says that "God is love." The Apostle Paul encouraged the Christians at Ephesus to grow in their knowledge of God "so that Christ may dwell in your hearts through faith. And I pray that you, being rooted and established in love, may have power, together with all the saints, to grasp how wide and long and high and deep is the love of Christ, and to know this love that surpasses knowledge— that you may be filled to the measure of all the fullness of God" (Eph. 3:17-19 NIV). If we are going to grow into victorious, vibrant believers, then it's imperative we get to know God in His great love.

An old '50s song says, "I wonder, wonder who... who wrote the book of love." Actually, that question was answered 2000 years ago. God wrote it, and it's called the Bible. It's God's great love letter to His children. Its main character is the Author and Creator of perfect love. He loved those that no one else cared for. He loved so much that it hurt. He loved even those who hated Him. He loved the lonely – the sick – the poor – the needy – and the rejected. He loved those filled with guilt, anger, bitterness, sin, and hate. Tens of thousands of books have been written about His great love. Multitudes of articles have been printed in an attempt to describe that great love.

The love of God which is found in Jesus is so great that Paul wanted that band of believers in Ephesus to know how long, high, wide, and deep it was. He wanted them to have a personal knowledge of the greatness of Christ's love. Paul knew that their growth in Christ was dependent on the knowledge of that love. We, too, must understand that victory in the Christian life is, to a great extent, related to our personal knowledge of God's love.

When I first came to know Christ, I was consumed with His love. I was overwhelmed with the fact that the Creator and Sustainer of the universe loved me. Wow! But even more incredible than that fact was how much He loved me. He loved me enough to allow His own Son, Jesus, to take the punishment for my sins. No one ever loved me like that. His love drove me to share the good news with anyone and everyone who would listen. However, as I grew in my faith and understanding of God, I began to notice that I was taking His love for granted. When I presumed on the love of God, I found myself dry and defeated. I need to be revived.

That's why I need to drink daily from the fountain of God's love. It's a spring that's everlasting – without beginning and end. The more I drink, the greater its flow. The higher I climb, the greater the thrill of the love of God. The deeper the trials, the sweeter His love tastes. The wider my circle of influence and acquaintances, the broader His embrace reaches. The longer I walk with Him, the farther I can see the love of God. His love is refreshing. It restores my soul – renews my laughter – and brightens my day. Perhaps that's why the 19th century evangelist, D. L. Moody, had painted in one of His the buildings the words, "God is love." He wanted everyone who visited Chicago and even the whole world to know that there is a God whose very essence is love.

Come and drink of that fountain! Taste and see that the Lord is good!

49

VICTORY OVER DARKNESS

Not long ago, a colleague and I were in Los Angeles, California. On Saturday evening, we visited an ethnic pastor who was originally from a Middle Eastern country. After discussing plans to reach that nation with the gospel of Christ, the pastor said, "I think that we really need to pray for Sammy. If God is going to use him in our nation, then Satan will surely attack him." The small group of believers gathered around me and prayed.

My friend and I then left his home at about 10:00 p.m. and headed for our hotel. We heard what sounded like five or six gunshots while driving back to our room. A pick-up truck immediately in front of us quickly stopped. We stopped behind him. We didn't know what was going on. So, we just sat there. All of a sudden the truck turned around in the middle of the road and sped away. We were still stopped and a couple of other cars had pulled up behind us and were also stopped. One car passed us. When he got about fifty yards ahead of us, gang members ran out into the street with guns. The last thing that I saw was the car door opening. We immediately turned around and sped off.

All I could think about on the way back to our hotel was how close we came to being shot. We were only 10-15 seconds away from being in the middle of gang shootings. Then I thought about the pastor who said just a few minutes before the incident, "I think that we really need to pray for Sammy. If God is going to use him in our nation, then Satan will surely attack him."

God has given me a special burden to go to the difficult areas of the world. I call them difficult because those who stand for Christ experience many difficulties when they share the gospel in those communities and nations. But I have been doing this long enough to know that God is our protector. He is our first and last line of defence. We don't have to be afraid. Satan may be "a roaring lion," but he's a toothless one. Psalm 91 is one of my favourite passages of Scripture because it gives a complete description of our victory.

"He who dwells in the shelter of the Most High
    will rest in the shadow of the Almighty.
I will say of the LORD, 'He is my refuge and my fortress,
    my God, in whom I trust.'
Surely he will save you from the fowler's snare
    and from the deadly pestilence.
He will cover you with his feathers,
    and under his wings you will find refuge;
    his faithfulness will be your shield and rampart.
You will not fear the terror of night,
    nor the arrow that flies by day,
nor the pestilence that stalks in the darkness,
    nor the plague that destroys at midday.
A thousand may fall at your side,
    ten thousand at your right hand,
    but it will not come near you.
You will only observe with your eyes
    and see the punishment of the wicked.

If you make the Most High your dwelling –
    even the LORD, who is my refuge –
then no harm will befall you,
    no disaster will come near your tent.
For he will command his angels concerning you
    to guard you in all your ways;
they will lift you up in their hands,
    so that you will not strike your foot against a stone.
You will tread upon the lion and the cobra;
    you will trample the great lion and the serpent.

"Because he loves me," says the LORD, "I will rescue him;
    I will protect him, for he acknowledges my name.
He will call upon me, and I will answer him;
    I will be with him in trouble,
    I will deliver him and honor him.
With long life will I satisfy him
    and show him my salvation."

I have watched God fulfil that promise in numerous countries around the world. I've walked into a revolution, the aftermath of an attempted genocide, and preached a major crusade in a war torn nation. I've been shot at, threatened, and run out of town for preaching the gospel. I've been arrested three times in nations that are hostile to Christianity. But every time, God has been faithful. Great is His faithfulness!

50

VICTORY THROUGH OUR CHOICES

His heart was on fire with the love of Christ. He wanted to share Jesus with all of his friends. He was gifted. Some might even say 'anointed'. As a young evangelist, hundreds of young people flocked to hear him preach, and many responded to his messages. It appeared that he had a bright future and that God's hand was mighty upon this young preacher.

Fast forward 33 years, and you discover that he's been married numerous times, with children from several different relationships. He's no longer in ministry. He has few if any deep relationships. His life goals from his youth are shattered. His life has become a sad story of defeat rather than a great testimony of God's grace and victory.

But my friend's story isn't that unusual. I've met many young men and women who began the race with the fire of God burning in their souls, but have finished defeated and saddened at what could have been a victorious run in life. What happens in such situations? Why do some of the most talented and gifted men and women of God find themselves defeated? Why do believers with such a passion for God end up drowning in the deep waters of sin and self?

There are certainly many legitimate answers to those questions. But perhaps the initial response must be that every Christian is faced with choices every day. Some of those choices are actually temptations. We must say 'no' to Satan's cunning ways and 'yes' to God. If we don't, we may find ourselves on a slippery path that leads to spiritual death and defeat.

The wrong choices in life may begin with a subtle look, a flirtatious smile or wink. We then begin making choices about fulfilling the lusts of our hearts. We act upon those things that would alienate us from God and drag us into defeat. The Bible says 'For all that is in the world, the lust of the flesh and the lust of the eyes and the boastful pride of life, is not from the Father, but is from the world' (1 John 2:16 NAS).

As long as we live in this world, we're going to have to make choices in three areas of life: (1) the lust of the flesh; (2) the lust of the eye; and (3) the boastful pride of life. Sin is no respecter of persons. If we choose any one of those areas, they will destroy us. How do we then overcome such temptations? How do we make the right decisions in life? How do we put our feet on the highway to holiness rather than the slippery slope of sin?

Our hearts must be set apart for God? We must passionately long to know and love Him more than we desire the passing pleasures of sin. We must hunger and thirst for His righteousness. When our hearts long to love Him, then we will have the strength to reject sin and embrace Christ. Jesus said, 'No one can serve two masters. Either he will hate the one and love the other, or he will be devoted to the one and despise the other' (Matt. 6:24 NIV). Every morning when you awaken, make a decision. Choose to love and serve Jesus. Before you ever place a foot outside your door, choose to passionately follow Christ. Make the right choice long before the temptation faces you. The right choices in life will lead to long-term victory. Choose Jesus. He is our victory.

51

A VICTORIOUS CHRISTMAS

I had spent 18 years celebrating Christmas without knowing the true meaning of Christmas. However, during the summer of 1965, I came to know God through Jesus. My life was completely changed. I had purpose and meaning. There was a sense of joy that permeated my entire life. My sins were forgiven, and the burden of guilt was removed from me. The Christian life was new to me. It was like an exciting adventure.

Even before I came to Christ, Christmas had always been a fun time. It was a season for parties, gift exchanges, and romance. But there was also a certain emptiness that accompanied the fun and parties. I recall one Christmas becoming so drunk that I tore up my car while driving. In the midst of the glitz and music, there was a sense of despair and confusion. Deep down I was lonely and hurting.

Then, my first real Christmas arrived. For the first time, I understood the true meaning of Christmas. I went to a party, and it was like I had a new set of eyes. All the drinking that people were doing seemed only to be an escape from the pain in their lives. Some friends wanted me to drink with them. But the alcohol had lost its appeal. I had joy within. I didn't need a synthetic joy produced from without.

I'll never forget that first Christmas Eve. My family always exchanged gifts on Christmas Eve. For the first time in my life, my dad gave me a Bible. I treasured it. After giving to each other our gifts, I received a phone call from a friend. He said, "Let's get together and give God a gift tonight in celebration of the birth of Jesus." That sounded great to me.

Four of us met together late in the evening and went looking for a church where we could pray. All the city churches were locked tight. Finally, we drove outside the city and found a small newly started church. It was open. We went inside and had a prayer meeting that lasted for about two hours. While we were praying, we all had this desire to give God a gift – but what do you give God? He owns everything. As we prayed, someone said, "God, I want to give you a soul during this Christmas season." All of us began to weep in agreement, "Yes, Lord, we want to bring someone to Jesus during these holidays."

I've learned since then that you cannot put a time on God. You can't just decide that you will lead someone to Christ during a certain period and that it will just automatically happen. God's Spirit must draw people to Christ. But we were young and new in the Lord. So, we prayed this way. On New Year's night, we went to the state capital building and had another prayer meeting. The state capital building in Baton Rouge, Louisiana used to have the lights turned on to make the sign of the cross.

We were on the side of a hill worshipping God when four other young men came up, staggering and singing. We were singing about Jesus, and they were singing about the devil. Each one of them had a bottle of vodka. They sat on one side of the hill, and we sat on the other side. Finally, one of my friends said, "Hey, God has brought these guys to us. Let's tell them about Jesus."

We did just that. About three hours later, those four

young men prayed to receive Christ. We were able to follow up with them and help them to grow in Christ. As I look back on Christmas, I think that first real Christmas was the best Christmas I've ever experienced. In all of your giving this Christmas, it might be good to pray and ask God what He would have you give Him. Merry Christmas!

52

FINISHING THE RACE

"You've done really well in your ministry. My prayer for you is that you finish well." Those words reverberated in the ears of the older minister as his son exhorted him. We would all do well to take heed to such encouragement. The Christian life can be more likened to a marathon rather than a sprint. God desires for us to finish well. Many begin the Christian life with great enthusiasm, but finish the race limping and some even crawling. God's desire is that we finish strong, running with endurance.

The author of Hebrews gave us the key to finishing the race of life well when he wrote, "therefore, since we are surrounded by such a great cloud of witnesses, let us throw off everything that hinders and the sin that so easily entangles, and let us run with perseverance the race marked out for us. Let us fix our eyes on Jesus, the author and perfecter of our faith, who for the joy set before Him endured the cross, scorning its shame, and sat down at the right hand of the throne of God" (Heb. 12:1,2 NIV).

We begin the Christian life looking unto Jesus. We continue it looking unto Jesus, and we can only conclude victoriously looking unto Jesus. Every step of the way we have to walk and live by faith. Men and women of old were victorious because they trusted Jesus to be their victory. They didn't have any special secret formula that caused them to be victorious. Their victory came from looking to Jesus as their source of strength. Paul struggled with sin. Abraham succumbed to fear. David fell into the arms of lust. Peter denied the Lord. All of them fell. But all got back up and walked by faith. They finished the race.

We must look to Jesus in the beginning of the race. In fact, we can't even begin the race without looking unto Jesus. That's where the Christian life begins. Then, it continues by looking unto Jesus and trusting Him. We are to trust Jesus daily for our victory in the same manner through which we came to Christ. That's the secret to victorious Christian living.

But we must also purpose in our hearts to look to Him, not only as the Author and Sustainer of our faith, but also the Perfecter of our faith. We must long to hear those words, "Well done, thou good and faithful servant." Jesus was faithful unto the end. Our commitment to Him must also be "unto the end." The Christian life is much more than an experience. It's a life. Early believers were called followers of "the Way." When they came to Christ, they adopted a whole new way of life. Often that way brought hardships and difficulties with it. Nevertheless, they were on a journey and were determined to complete that journey. Some were fed to lions. Others were burned at stakes. But they looked unto Jesus. They finished well.

Why don't you spend some time placing your focus upon Jesus? Look unto Him. If there is anything unlike Jesus in your life, then confess and allow God to cleanse you of it. Look unto Jesus. Ask God to work mightily within you to conform you into the image of Jesus. Begin this next year more like Jesus than you began this past year. Look unto Jesus. Determine that you will finish the race looking unto Jesus. Say goodbye to this year and hello to next year by looking unto Jesus.

Sammy Tippit can be contacted
in the following ways:

Sammy Tippit Ministries

P.O. Box 781767

San Antonio, Texas 78278
U.S.A.

Email: stm@sammytippit.org

Web: http://www.sammytippit.org

Tel. - 1-210-492-7501

Fax - 1-210-492-4522

PERSONAL DATA:
DR. SAMMY TIPPIT –
EVANGELIST OF PEACE

At the beginning of this new century, international evangelist and author Sammy Tippit is emerging as a leading voice among the nations. He is currently preaching some of the largest evangelistic meetings in the world. He has proclaimed God's message of peace in stadiums in war-torn Burundi, met with government and religious leaders shortly after the attempted genocide in Rwanda, and brought hope to persecuted believers in the former Soviet-bloc nations. Tippit preached a historic evangelistic meeting in Addis Ababa, Ethiopia in March 1999, with over 300,000 people attending in four days. In May of that same year, he preached in Maracana, the world's largest stadium, located in Rio de Janeiro. Not only did thousands come to Christ, but the event was attended and supported by the governor, vice governor, and mayor of the city and state. In the last 30 years of ministry, Tippit has proclaimed the gospel in more than 55 countries throughout the world.

The following is personal data concerning Sammy Tippit:

- Born in 1947 in Baton Rouge, Louisiana.
- Participated in study group from Louisiana at the United Nations in 1964. He was awarded "Most Outstanding Youth Speaker in North America."
- Graduated from Istrouma High School in 1965.
- Experienced his "conversion" to Christianity and call to ministry during August 1965.
- Married to Debara "Tex" Sirman on June 8, 1968. The Tippits have two children, Dave (27) and Renee (23).
- Ordained as a Southern Baptist Minister in 1968.
- Founded evangelistic organization, God's Love In Action, in 1970.
- Began street ministry in high-crime district of Chicago in 1970, working with gangs, drug addicts, and troubled youth. Became known as leader of "Jesus Movement" in Chicago.

- Traveled internationally to Germany for evangelistic youth rallies in 1971.
- Collaborated with Jerry Jenkins (writer of Billy Graham's best-selling autobiography, *Just As I Am,* and author of the best-selling fiction series, *Left Behind*) in 1972 on the biography of Sammy's early life.
- Infiltrated "Communist Youth World Fest" in 1973 and shared the gospel among the 100,000 youth gathered.
- Traveled extensively in communist-dominated countries doing evangelistic ministry from 1973–1988.
- Preached first evangelistic stadium crusade in the history of Romania in May 1990.
- Preached first Republic-wide evangelistic meetings in Moldova in September 1990.
- Preached first evangelistic stadium meetings in numerous cities throughout Russia, Ukraine, Romania, Albania, and Moldova.
- Preached first public outdoor evangelistic meetings in Mongolia in 1992.
- Received an honorary doctorate from Lancaster Bible College in 1993.
- Preached evangelistic meeting in Rwanda shortly after the attempted genocide in 1994 and worked with leaders to bring Hutus and Tutsis together in a spirit of reconciliation.
- Preached in war-torn Burundi and met with peace negotiators in 1998.
- Preached to 300,000 in four days in Ethiopia in 1999.
- Preached evangelistic meetings in Maracana, world's largest stadium, in Rio de Janeiro in May 1999.
- Authored and co-authored twelve books which have been translated into numerous languages.

Christian Focus Publications publishes biblically-accurate books for adults and children. The books in the adult range are published in three imprints.

Christian Heritage contains classic writings from the past.

Christian Focus contains popular works including biographies, commentaries, doctrine, and Christian living.

Mentor focuses on books written at a level suitable for Bible College and seminary students, pastors, and others; the imprint includes commentaries, doctrinal studies, examination of current issues, and church history.

For a free catalogue of all our titles, please write to
Christian Focus Publications,
Geanies House, Fearn,
Ross-shire, IV20 1TW, Great Britain

For details of our titles visit us on our web site
http://www.christianfocus.com